WRITING
FROM START TO FINISH
A SIX-STEP GUIDE

KATE GRENVILLE

ALLEN&UNWIN

Allen & Unwin
83 Alexander Street
Crows Nest NSW 2065
Australia
Phone: (61 2) 8425 0100
Fax: (61 2) 9906 2218
Email: info@allenandunwin.com
Web: www.allenandunwin.com

National Library of Australia
Cataloguing-in-Publication entry:

Grenville, Kate, 1950–.
   Writing from start to finish: a six-step guide.

   Includes index.
   ISBN 1 86508 514 6.

   1. Creative writing. 2. Essay—Authorship.
   3. English language—Rhetoric. I. Title.

808.042

Text design by Simon Paterson
Illustrations by Fiona Katauskas
Set in 10/15 pt Stempel Schneidler by Bookhouse, Sydney
Printed by Griffin Press, South Australia

10 9 8 7 6 5 4 3 2

CONTENTS

Introduction

What makes writing hard?

Writing sounds simple—you start with an attention-grabbing first sentence, then you move on to some really interesting stuff in the middle, and then you bring it all together at the end.

The trouble is, how do you think up that attention-grabbing first sentence? Where do you go to find that really interesting stuff? What do you do if your mind is as blank as the paper you're staring at?

Sometimes writing happens the way it does in the movies. You sit down, chew the end of the pen for a while, then you get inspired and something fantastic comes out. This is great when it happens, and if all your writing's like that, well, hey, you can stop reading now. You don't need this book.

This book is about what to do when you've chewed the pen down to the ink and you still haven't got any ideas.

How this book helps

This book is different from many other 'how to write' books because it reverses the usual order you do things in. Many books about writing suggest you think out in advance what you're going to write. After you've thought out your piece, you write it.

This sounds logical and sensible. It works for some people all of the time. It works for some people some of the time. But it doesn't work at all, ever, for many people, myself included.

Mainly, this is because of that little voice we've all got in our head that says, 'That's no good, stupid!'. The trick to writing is to find a

Most people don't find writing easy.

way of making that little voice shut up long enough for you to get something down on paper.

The way I suggest you approach writing is to start by letting your mind roam around the topic in a free-form way. You make notes and write little bits and pieces, exploring many different ways into the topic.

When you've got a good collection of these bits, you pick over them for what you might be able to use, and you start to put them in some kind of order. As you do this, more ideas will come. Gradually, this evolves into your finished piece of writing.

The advantage of doing it this way is that you never have to make ideas appear out of thin air. Even if your bits and pieces aren't brilliant, they are something—if only something to react against.

It also means that the process of *creating* and the process of *judging* are separate. Once you've got something written, you can invite that nasty little voice back in to evaluate what you've got and make changes.

Instead of being caught up *inside* the machinery of your own thinking, you can stand *outside* it, and see the process happening one step at a time.

> Writing evolves, it doesn't just arrive.

> Write first, judge later.

Can anyone learn to write?

Experienced writers do a lot of these steps in their head, so fast they often aren't even aware they're doing them. It looks as if something intuitive and magic is happening—as if their brains are working differently. I don't think that is so—but I think they're going through the steps so fast and so seamlessly, it looks like a leap rather than a plod. It's like driving—experienced drivers shift gears without having to think about it. Learner drivers, though, have to think consciously about it and practise gear shifting until it becomes automatic.

No one's born knowing how to write—but it's a skill that most people can learn, and the more you do it, the easier it becomes.

How the six steps work

This book is based on the idea that you can use the same process for any kind of writing. Short stories, essays, reports—they all look very different, and they're doing different jobs, but you can go about them all in the same way using these same six steps:

1. Getting ideas (in no particular order).
2. Choosing (selecting the ideas you think will be most useful).
3. Outlining (putting these ideas into the best order—making a plan).
4. Drafting (doing a first draft from beginning to end, without going back).
5. Revising (cutting, adding or moving parts of this draft where necessary).
6. Editing (proofreading for grammar, spelling and paragraphs).

I know these six steps work because I follow them every time I sit down to write.

In the pages ahead, you'll find a chapter for each step, containing:

 information **about** the step—how to do it;

 an **example** of the step—over the course of the book, these examples evolve into a completed short story and a completed essay;

 a **doing it** section where you can apply what you've learned in the chapter.

You can just look at the chapters you need at the moment. If you want to learn how to write an essay, for example, you can read the 'about' section, then skip ahead to the 'example' and 'doing it' sections for essay writing. Look for these icons in the bottom corner of the page.

Writing gets easier with practice.

Remember:
Go
Cook
One
Dreadful
Raw
Egg.

You don't have to read through this book from beginning to end.

At the end of the book there are a few other sections that should be useful:

★ a summary of the different types of texts and their requirements;

★ a user-friendly guide to some of the most common grammar problems;

★ a quick reference to the six steps for exam revision.

Writing assignments

There seem to be so many different kinds of writing: novels, poems, short stories, scripts, letters, essays, reports, reviews, instructions…all quite different. But they're all *writing*. They all have the basic aim of getting ideas from one brain into another.

Any piece of writing will be trying to do at least one of the following things:

> ★ **Entertain**—it doesn't necessarily make the readers laugh, but it at least *engages their feelings* in some way.
>
> ★ **Inform**—it tells the reader about something.
>
> ★ **Persuade**—it tries to convince the reader of something.

In the real world these purposes overlap. But a good place to start writing is to ask: What is the basic thing I want this piece of writing to do?

Writing to entertain

Think what it's like to be a reader—you can be entertained (emotionally gripped) by something very serious, even sad, as well as by something funny. An exciting plot can involve your emotions, too, by creating feelings of suspense. Writing that involves emotions can also be reflective and contemplative.

Writing to entertain generally takes the form of so-called 'imaginative writing' or 'creative writing' (of course, all writing requires some imagination and creativity). Examples of imaginative writing are novels, stories, poems, song lyrics, plays and screenplays.

Sometimes imaginative writing disguises itself as a 'true story' for added effect. For example, *The Secret Diary of Adrian Mole* by Sue Townsend disguises itself as a journal, while *Dear Venny, Dear Saffron*

Trying to put writing in categories can make you crazy, but it gets you thinking about what you're trying to do.

For imaginative writing you can make things up.

by Gary Crew and Libby Hathorn disguises itself as letters. As readers, though, we know that they're not really journals or letters—these are just devices the writer has used to make the writing more entertaining.

Writing to inform

These kinds of writing can also be 'entertaining' in the sense that they're a good read. But entertaining the reader isn't their main purpose—that's just a bonus.

Examples of writing to inform are newspaper articles, scientific or business reports, instructions or procedures, and essays for school and university.

Writing to persuade

This includes advertisements, some newspaper and magazine articles, and some types of essay. This type of writing might include your opinion, but as part of a logical case backed up with evidence, rather than just as an expression of your feelings.

I mentioned above that imaginative writing occasionally pretends to be a true story, but if you're writing to inform or persuade, you shouldn't make things up.

If you're writing to inform or persuade, don't make things up!

Understanding assignments

Sometimes you're free to write whatever you like, but at school or university you'll generally be given a specific writing assignment. This could be an imaginative writing assignment, an essay, or some other kind of writing task. Decoding the words of the assignment so that you give your teacher or lecturer exactly what he or she wants is part of your job as a writer. There are two clues embedded in every assignment that will help you crack the code:

Reading teachers' minds: What do they really want?

★ the **task word**; and
★ the **limiting word**.

Task words

The **task word** is usually the verb in the assignment—the word that tells you what to do. It might be something like: 'discuss'; 'describe'; 'write about'; or 'compare'.

For example: ***Discuss*** *the poem 'Mending Wall' by Robert Frost.* Or: ***Write about*** *your childhood.*

Limiting words

The **limiting word** (or words) narrows the assignment in some way. For example: *Discuss **the use of imagery** in the poem 'Mending Wall' by Robert Frost.*

Or: *Write about **the most embarrassing incident** of your childhood.*

Sometimes, writing assignments have a sneaky hidden agenda. They seem to be asking for an imaginative response, but they're also looking for how much you know about a particular subject.

For example: *Write a letter to the editor of a publishing company, recommending that the company publish the work of Robert Frost.* The hidden agenda is to show how much you know, in as much detail as possible, about Robert Frost's poems. The 'letter' format is just fancy packaging for good old information and argument.

Two kinds of writing assignments

In this book, we'll look in detail at two of the most common kinds of writing assignment:

★ imaginative writing assignments;
★ essay assignments.

Imaginative writing assignments

For information about other kinds of writing assignments, see page 189.

Assignments for imaginative writing commonly give you something that acts as a trigger for your imagination. For example:

★ Look at this photograph and write a piece responding to it.

★ Write a piece that begins with a young child waking, sitting up in bed saying, 'It's my birthday! and promptly bursting into tears.

★ Write a piece based on the theme 'State of the Art'.

Others give you part of the story ready-made—the title, the opening or the end.

★ Use this as the title of a piece of writing: 'The Very Worst'.

★ Use this as the first sentence of a piece of writing: 'The car coughed, sputtered, choked and died'.

★ Use this as the final sentence of a piece of writing: 'High up in the sky, a jet drew a long, soft line of vapour through the unclouded blue'.

Whatever form the assignment takes, it is asking you to write a piece that will 'entertain' your readers—that is, engage their feelings.

Essay assignments

These assignments invite you to show what you know about a subject.

Essays generally ask you to do one of four things:

★ They might ask for straight **information**, arranged in some logical order: an explanatory essay or report. For example: *What are the themes of 'Mending Wall' by Robert Frost?*

★ They might ask you to **discuss different points of view** about a subject: to present one side, then the other and finally come down on one side. For example: *Robert Frost's poem 'Mending Wall' is his best poem. Discuss.*

★ They might ask you to **argue for a particular point of view**—to make a case for **one side** of an argument. For example: *Robert Frost's poem 'Mending Wall' is his best poem. Do you agree or disagree? Give reasons for your answer.*

★ Or they might ask you to **compare or contrast** several different things. For example: *Robert Frost's poem 'Mending Wall' expresses the same themes as some of his other poems, but in a different way. Discuss.*

If only it was this easy...

Writing assignments

To show the process of writing from start to finish, I'm going to set myself two writing assignments and work through them using the six steps.

Imaginative writing assignment

I've given myself this assignment:

> Write a piece with the title 'Steep Learning Curve'.

The task words here are 'write a piece'. This is a very open-ended phrase giving me a clue that I can approach the assignment in whatever way I choose—it can be a poem or a play or a story.

The limiting words are 'with the title "Steep Learning Curve"'. This means that what I write about has to have something to do with a steep learning curve, but the exact kind of learning curve is up to me.

These clues suggest that the purpose of this piece will be to *entertain*. I'll work towards a piece of **imaginative writing** in the form of a short story.

Essay assignment

This is the assignment I've set myself:

> 'Every story is a journey towards self-discovery.' Using a novel you've read this year as an example, show why you agree or disagree with this statement.

The task words here are 'show why you agree or disagree'. This clue tells me I should try to *persuade* the reader that I'm right in agreeing—or disagreeing—with the statement.

The limiting words are 'using a novel you've read this year as an example'. This is a clue to write about just one book, and to use examples from it to back up what I'm saying. In doing this, I'll also be *informing* the reader of what the book is about. I'll work towards an **essay** of the kind required at school and university.

These examples will develop step-by-step through the book.

Writing assignments

1 Why am I writing this piece?

Ask yourself:

★ Am I being asked to write a piece that will **entertain** my reader (that is, keep them interested by getting their feelings involved, probably by making things up)?

★ Am I being asked to write a piece that will **inform** my reader (that is, tell them facts about something in the real world)?

★ Am I being asked to write a piece that will **persuade** my reader (that is, put forward an argument and convince them it's the correct one)?

Hint...think about the purpose of the piece.

2 What's the task of this assignment?

★ What is the **task word** in this assignment? (Am I being asked to discuss, describe or compare, or something else?)

★ What is the **limiting word** or phrase? Is the assignment asking me to limit my piece to just one part of a larger subject?

★ Is there a **hidden agenda** in this assignment? (Is it presented as an imaginative task, but also asks for information?)

Hint...look at the verb in the assignment.

3 What kind of writing should I do here?

★ Are there clues that tell me what form the writing should take (to write the piece as an essay, as a short story, as a newspaper report)?

Hint...some assignments let you choose, others don't.

Recap

Now that you know what the assignment is asking you to do, you need ideas. How do you get those ideas? The next chapter is about several tried-and-true ways.

STEP ONE

Getting ideas

WRITING'S a bit like fishing — you NEVER KNOW what You'll caTcH....

What's in STEP ONE

About getting ideas

Ideas come from lots of places, but the one place they never, ever come from is a sheet of blank paper. Blank paper will never lead to anything better than more blank paper. That's why, if I had any rules for writing (which I don't), my first and last rule would be: *Anything is better than a blank page.*

Getting ideas isn't usually a matter of having one giant brainstorm. More often, it's a matter of gradually accumulating a little idea here, another little idea there. Eventually they all add up.

Here are four foolproof ways to get some words down on that blank page:

★ making a list;

★ making a cluster diagram;

★ researching or independent investigation;

★ freewriting.

Making a list (or 'brainstorming' or 'think-tanking') is the best way I know to get started with a piece of writing. Your mind can flit around the topic quickly. You don't have to write a list in sentences, so you don't get bogged down trying to think of the right words. You can just write anything that comes to mind.

Making a cluster diagram is really just another kind of list, but one that develops into little clusters of like-minded ideas. If yours is one of those brains that works best visually, a cluster diagram might be a user-friendly way to start writing.

Researching or independent investigation means finding some information to use in your writing. The obvious place to do research is in books, but you can also do it on the Net, from videos and by gathering your own information first-hand (doing interviews, conducting experiments, etc.).

Freewriting (or 'speedwriting' or 'free-associating') just means non-stop talking onto the page. Because you can't stop to think, your unconscious gets to have a go.

Even a dumb idea can lead to a better idea.

They sound simple and they are—but they work!

What stops ideas?

The Voice of Doom

The hardest thing about getting ideas is that little voice in your head that tells you all your ideas are no good. We all have that voice. I've been a professional writer for twenty years and I still get it every time I sit down to write.

I don't think you can make that voice go away. If you wait for it to go away—if you wait until you feel happy with your ideas—you'll wait a lifetime and never get anything done. The thing to do is to *go on in spite of it*. Speak firmly to it. 'Okay,' you can say: 'It's no good. I won't argue about that. But I'll just keep going anyway. Laugh all you want.'

'Inspiration'

You can't force ideas. The best ones often come when you're not trying to control your brain too much. They often feel as if they have come out of nowhere.

They haven't really come from nowhere, though—they've come out of your brain—but out of the unconscious part. The unconscious is like the hidden two-thirds of an iceberg—it supports everything else, but you can't see it.

What happens when you get an 'inspiration' is just that the conscious, thinking part of your brain has switched off for a minute, and the unconscious has switched on. The unconscious is a writer's best friend.

The unconscious goes on strike if you try to tell it what to do or if you criticise it. This means to get ideas you have to let your mind roam wherever it wants to. Once your unconscious has given you some ideas, your conscious mind can take over again.

Premature planning

It's true that when you start to write a piece, you should have a plan. But *getting ideas* isn't the same as *writing a piece*. There's a time to think and plan (in this book, that time is during Step Three), and a time to let your mind wander freely, gathering all kinds of ideas.

Writer's block

There's a lot of melodrama around the idea of writer's block, but it's not a terminal illness. It just means that you've come to the end of one path of ideas. That's okay—you go off on another one. Instead of trying to force a path *through* the wall, you go *around* it.

One thing that helps is to remind yourself that no one else is going to read any of this. Step One is your own private notes to yourself—like an artist's rough sketches. It also helps to remind yourself that *everything* goes through a stage where it looks hopeless. Making toffee, learning to rollerblade, painting your bedroom—there's always a moment when that little voice says, 'This is never going to work'. But just on the other side of that moment is the breakthrough.

It also helps to remember that you have had ideas in the past. This suggests you might have more in the future. Think about a good idea you've had in the past—not necessarily about writing. How did you get the idea for that Mother's Day present your mum liked so much? How did the idea for the Self-Adjusting Shoelace Doer-Upper come to you? Is there a state of mind, or a set of circumstances that makes it easier for you to think of good ideas?

Thinking that you have to write a masterpiece is a sure way to get writer's block. None of the things we'll do in Step One will look like a masterpiece. Don't let that worry you. This isn't the step where we write the masterpiece. This is the step where we think up a whole lot of ideas. Writing the masterpiece comes later.

'Writer's block' is a normal part of writing.

Beware of the pressure to write a masterpiece!

The next section is about getting ideas for imaginative writing. If you're looking for help with an essay, skip ahead to page 28.

Getting ideas for imaginative writing

The aim of a piece of imaginative writing is to **entertain** the reader, so that means I'll be trying to think of **entertaining** ideas.

That's a big ask. Very few people can think of entertaining ideas straight off. So—I'll work up to it. I'll start by asking my brain to think up any old ideas. One idea leads to another and sooner or later they'll get more entertaining. As I mentioned on page 11, there are at least four good ways to come up with 'any old ideas'.

Writing isn't easy—so start with something simple.

Making a list

A **list** is the easiest, least threatening way to start writing. Start by working out what is the single most important word or phrase in the assignment. This is the **key word**. Write that at the top of a blank page and list anything that comes into your head about it.

Making a cluster diagram

Another way of making a list is to do it in the form of a **cluster diagram**.

Instead of having the assignment at the top of the page, you write the key word from the assignment in the *middle* of the page. You put down ideas as they come to you, and if they connect to an idea you've already put down, you group them together. The aim is to form clusters of linked ideas.

The act of clustering ideas often seems to make it easier for them to flow. Also, your ideas can jump from cluster to cluster, adding a bit here, a bit there.

Researching

Another name for **research** is **independent investigation** because
what it means is going and finding out something about the subject
yourself. There are two reasons to do research for a piece of
creative writing:

★ as a way of **finding ideas**;

★ as a way of **finding interesting details** to develop ideas
you already have.

A lot of imaginative writing gets done without any research at all.
But research can make a dull story come to life—it can add vivid
details and make it more believable.

Research for imaginative writing can be about a location (John Marsden, for example, drew on real places and stories for *Tomorrow, When the War Began*). It can be about a historical period (Colleen McCullough does a lot of historical research for her books about ancient Rome). Or it can delve into technical information (such as in Michael Crichton's *Jurassic Park*).

Research might also take the form of direct personal investigation—asking your grandmother what life was like when she was a child, for example, or gathering information about your family tree.

Writers often keep a notebook for their research—if you see an odd-shaped cloud or overhear something peculiar on the bus, you put in it your notebook. Later, when you're writing, you can go through the notebook and see if that cloud or that overheard comment can go in your story. In all these cases, the writer is making use of the fact that truth is often stranger than fiction (and more interesting, too).

Carry a notebook with you and write things down **straight away**. A few words will do.

Freewriting

Freewriting is just thinking on paper. It's a good way to let the unconscious give you ideas because it lets you access your memory, your experiences, your knowledge, your fantasies...things you didn't even know you had stored away in your head.

The idea is to switch the brain off while keeping the pen moving across the paper. It's important not to plan what you're writing, or the ideas will stop flowing. It's also important not to stop and think. For freewriting the whole idea is *not* to think.

I know that it's hard to stop the brain thinking and planning, because we've all been taught to do that. However, switching the thinking-and-planning brain off for a while is also something you can learn, and like other things it gets easier with practice. (And don't worry, you'll switch it on again in Step Two.)

Getting ideas for imaginative writing

Making a list

To remind you, the imaginative writing assignment I've given myself is:

> *Write a piece with the title 'Steep Learning Curve'.*

The most important word here seems to be 'learning', so I'll begin with that and start listing everything that comes into my mind about 'learning'— any kind of learning. Here's what comes out.

LEARNING	Learning tennis
	Hitting balls over fence
	Huge swing, then miss
	Jeff Jackson laughing at me
Learning to read	*** ← Another dead end
Learning to tell the time	
Learning to swim	Learning French
*** ← Can't think of anything else	Learning lists of words by heart
The Olympic Pool	Embarrassing trying to say the
Blue water	words out loud
Little white hexagonal tiles	Other kids seemed to be getting
Dad holding me under the chest	it okay
Don't let go, don't let go	Me the only dummie
Funny echoing noises ← Brain's stopped!	
Feeling of water up nose	
***	

There's nothing brilliant here, but I've got examples of three different kinds of learning: learning to swim, learning tennis, and learning French. That means I've got three ideas about the assignment now, where two minutes ago I had a blank sheet of paper.

Making a cluster diagram

I start with the key word in the middle of a page:

To get myself going I use a few ideas from my first list. As I do this, new ideas start coming.

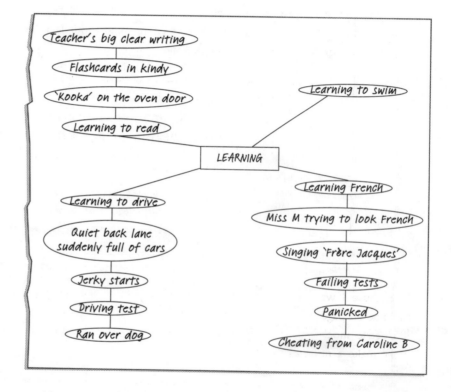

Messy, isn't it? Making a cluster diagram is one time when it's good to be messy. It means the ideas are flowing.

Researching

First, I'll use research to **find some ideas**.

In a psychology book I look through the index for the word 'learning' and come to an entry called 'Conditioned learning'. I skim through until this bit catches my eye:

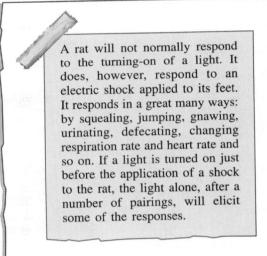

A rat will not normally respond to the turning-on of a light. It does, however, respond to an electric shock applied to its feet. It responds in a great many ways: by squealing, jumping, gnawing, urinating, defecating, changing respiration rate and heart rate and so on. If a light is turned on just before the application of a shock to the rat, the light alone, after a number of pairings, will elicit some of the responses.

Because I was thinking about French classes while I was writing my list back on page 17, I've got a fellow feeling for those rats. No one gave us electric shocks in French classes, but sometimes it felt like that.

I'll make a note about it:

Learning French as bad as electric shocks.
Learned to dread Wednesdays and Fridays—French days.
Tried to be invisible, avoid teacher's eye.

Second, I'll use research to **develop some ideas** I already have.

I could research 'learning to swim' (perhaps by going to a swimming pool and watching kids learning to swim). I could research 'learning tennis' (perhaps by watching some kids learning tennis). As it happens, my old French textbook is close at hand, so I'll use that to research 'learning French'. Was it really as hard to learn as it had seemed back when I was thirteen? When I get to this bit, I decide it was:

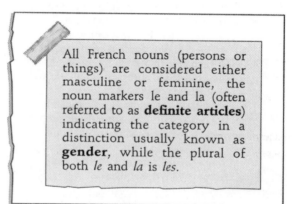

All French nouns (persons or things) are considered either masculine or feminine, the noun markers le and la (often referred to as **definite articles**) indicating the category in a distinction usually known as **gender**, while the plural of both *le* and *la* is *les*.

Freewriting

I write the words 'Steep Learning Curve' at the top of a sheet of paper, set a timer for three minutes, and start writing. Here's what comes out:

> Learning—hard and embarrassing, you can't do it, you feel stupid. Worse with people who already know how to do it. Now what? I can't think of anything else to write. I don't think this is working French was the worst, it didn't make sense. Maison meant house, I could learn that, a bit like mansion. But what about the 'le' and 'la' business? How were you supposed to remember that—two different words for 'the'? Why? Why some 'feminine' and some 'masculine'? I asked Miss M—Why is 'leg' feminine and 'foot' masculine. She gave me that 'what a dummie' look. The whole class staring at me. Now I've run out of things to cheated. Copied from Caroline B next to me. She tried to stop me—sloped her page away and hid it behind her hand. Maybe I really wanted to be found cheating, so someone would rescue me.

Suddenly thought of something else.

Remembered something I hadn't thought of for years.

I didn't consciously *decide* to freewrite about French—but it was in my mind from doing the research, so that's what came out.

IMAGINATIVE WRITING

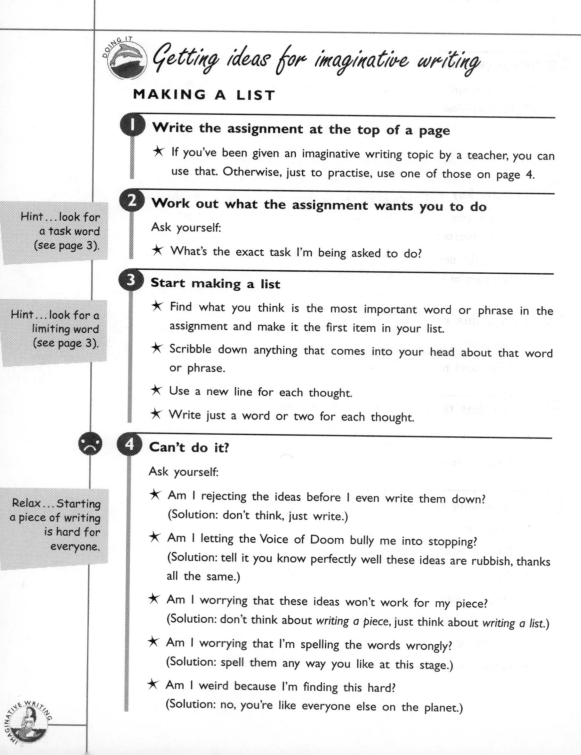

Getting ideas for imaginative writing

MAKING A LIST

1 Write the assignment at the top of a page

★ If you've been given an imaginative writing topic by a teacher, you can use that. Otherwise, just to practise, use one of those on page 4.

2 Work out what the assignment wants you to do

Ask yourself:

★ What's the exact task I'm being asked to do?

Hint...look for a task word (see page 3).

3 Start making a list

★ Find what you think is the most important word or phrase in the assignment and make it the first item in your list.

★ Scribble down anything that comes into your head about that word or phrase.

★ Use a new line for each thought.

★ Write just a word or two for each thought.

Hint...look for a limiting word (see page 3).

4 Can't do it?

Ask yourself:

★ Am I rejecting the ideas before I even write them down?
(Solution: don't think, just write.)

★ Am I letting the Voice of Doom bully me into stopping?
(Solution: tell it you know perfectly well these ideas are rubbish, thanks all the same.)

★ Am I worrying that these ideas won't work for my piece?
(Solution: don't think about *writing a piece*, just think about *writing a list*.)

★ Am I worrying that I'm spelling the words wrongly?
(Solution: spell them any way you like at this stage.)

★ Am I weird because I'm finding this hard?
(Solution: no, you're like everyone else on the planet.)

Relax... Starting a piece of writing is hard for everyone.

5 **When your list fills the page, you can stop and read it over**

If this list doesn't look like enough, don't panic. There are lots of other ways to get ideas—keep reading for some more.

MAKING A CLUSTER DIAGRAM

1 **Find the key word or words**

★ Make a box in the middle of the page and write the key word (the most important word) of the assignment in it.

★ Take your time making it look nice, because while you're busy doing that, part of your brain is actually thinking about the assignment.

2 **Draw a line out from the box**

Ask yourself:

★ What does this make me think of?

3 **Write that thought down**

★ Wrap it in a little idea bubble.

★ Attach it to the box the key word is in.

4 **Keep asking questions about the key word**

Ask yourself:

★ Does it make me remember something that once happened to me?

★ Does it make me think of another word?

★ Does it make me think of its opposite?

★ Does it make me think of something that seems to have nothing to do with the topic?

★ Does it make me think of a particular person, or place, or incident?

Hint...just put down the first thing that comes into your head.

Hint...no matter what you think of it, write it down anyway.

5 **Ask questions about the idea bubbles, too**

Ask yourself:

★ Does this make me remember something else?

★ Does this make me wonder about something, or start to imagine or make up something?

6 **Getting stuck?**

Ask yourself:

Hint...a messy cluster diagram is a good cluster diagram.

★ Am I pre-judging my ideas?
(Solution: don't judge them till later.)

★ Am I worrying that I'm going off into irrelevant ideas?
(Solution: worry later about whether they're relevant.)

★ Am I getting bogged down repeating myself?
(Solution: go back to the key word, or to one of the bubbles, and start again.)

★ Is my diagram all lopsided?
(Solution: relax—lopsided is fine for a cluster diagram.)

RESEARCHING

1 **Choose something from your list to find more information about**

Ask yourself:

★ Is there a person, a place or an event that I can find out more about?

★ Is there a general idea or concept that I can fill in with specific details?

2 **Start looking for information**

Ask yourself:

★ Is there a reference book I can look up (a dictionary, encyclopedia, atlas…)?

★ Is there a book about the subject (either non-fiction or fiction)?

★ Can I find sites about this on the Net?

★ Is there a film or video about this?

> Hint…
> researching's like fishing—the bigger your net, the more fish you'll catch.

3 **Decide whether to research personally**

Ask yourself:

★ Is there someone I can interview about this (either an individual or a group)?

★ Can I investigate it by observing it myself (going and having a good *look* at what I'm researching)?

★ Can I investigate it by experiencing it directly (doing it myself)?

IMAGINATIVE WRITING

4 **How to tell when you've found something useful**

Ask yourself:

★ Did I think 'Wow, that's really funny/weird/revolting/incredible'?

★ Did I find something sticking in my mind, even something I don't think is 'relevant'?

★ Did I find some specific examples of something I've been thinking about in general terms? (For example, if you were thinking about 'flowers' and now you've got 'daisies, roses, flannel flowers, lilies...')

★ Did I find details about a person or a place?

★ Did I hear a way of speaking or some other sound?

★ Can I understand how something feels from the inside now that I've tried doing it?

5 **Make a quick note of what you find and where it's located**

For more on note-taking, see page 30.

6 **What if you can't find anything?**

★ Leave it and go on to the next way of gathering ideas. Later, when the piece is further advanced, you might see what you need to research.

FREEWRITING

1 **Get some kind of timer and set it for five minutes**

★ This is so you don't have to keep checking how many minutes you've done.

2 **Write the main words of the topic at the top of the page**

★ Keep writing without stopping.

★ If you can't think of anything else to write and you want to stop, don't.

> Hint...keep the pen moving across the paper, no matter what comes out.

3 **What if I really can't keep going?**

Ask yourself:

★ Am I trying to plan in advance what I'll say?
(Solution: let each word suggest the next one—just go forward one word at a time.)

★ Am I worried about writing something silly?
(Solution: write something *really* silly. Then you can stop worrying about it.)

★ Do I keep wanting to stop and read what I've written?
(Solution: promise yourself you can do that, but not till the timer goes off.)

★ Am I going round in circles saying the same thing over and over?
(Solution: take a fresh page and give yourself a run-up with one of these writing starters:
'One day, I...'   'The thing about [key word] is...'
'One incident I remember about [key word] is...'
'The best/worst [key word] memory I have is...')

> Try 'I can't think of anything to write. This is the silliest thing I've ever done', etc. Eventually your brain will come up with something else.

4 **Think automatic writing**

It's a Zen kind of thing—just let whatever comes, come.

> Relax... the Great Writing isn't supposed to happen till Step Six.

The next section is about getting ideas for an essay. If you want to go on with imaginative writing, skip ahead to Step Two (page 47).

Getting ideas for an essay

For an essay, your aim is to **persuade** or **inform** your readers about the topic, so you want to end up with ideas that will persuade or inform.

Where do you start? Should you find out about the topic by doing research first? But how do you know what you need to research? Like so much of writing, it's a chicken-and-egg sort of thing.

The thing is not to worry about whether you've got a chicken or an egg. You need both and it doesn't matter which you start with. The place to start is to put down everything you already know or think about the topic. Once you get that in a line, you'll see where to go next.

Don't worry yet about your theme or your structure. You're not writing an essay yet—you're just exploring. The more you explore, the more ideas you'll get, and the more ideas you have, the better your essay will be.

Making a list

Writing an essay takes several different kinds of skills, but the first one is easy. We can all write a list. Start the list by writing down the most important word or phrase (the key word) from the assignment, then putting down every thought that comes to you about it.

Making a cluster diagram

A cluster diagram is really just another kind of list, but instead of listing straight down the page, you list in clusters around a key word. Think of the spokes of a wheel radiating out from the hub.

Something about the physical layout of a cluster diagram often makes it easier for ideas to start flowing. You can jump around from cluster to cluster, adding a thought here and a thought there.

It doesn't matter where you start, as long as you get something on paper.

A cluster diagram is also known as brainstorming or an idea tree.

Researching

When you write an essay, you're usually expected to find out what other people have already thought about the subject. Your own ideas are important too, but they should be built on a foundation of what's gone before. You don't have to reinvent the wheel.

Since most essays rely on this kind of foundation, you need to know how to do it properly. I'll take a moment here to talk about how to research (otherwise known as independent investigation).

Research is about getting some hard information on your subject: actual facts, actual figures. The sad thing about research is that usually only a small percentage of it ends up in your final draft. But like the hidden nine-tenths of an iceberg, it's got to be there to hold up the bit you can see.

You often research several times during the writing process. The first time you mightn't know exactly what you'll be writing about, so research will be fairly broad-based. As the essay starts to take shape, you'll have narrowed the topic down. At that stage you might research again to find specific details.

How do you research?

First you have to find your source of information.

You might look at books, journals, videos, newspapers, on the Internet, on CD-ROM. You go to reference books like dictionaries and encyclopedias.

You might also do your own research: interviewing people, conducting an experiment, doing a survey. In the case of my topic, reading the novels themselves is research (the novels are 'primary sources'), and so is finding anything that critics or reviewers might have said about them (these are 'secondary sources').

Research—you need it, even if it ends up **between** the lines, not **on** them.

Research is only as trustworthy as its source.

Research is only useful if you can say where you found it.

More information on how to acknowledge other people's work can be found on page 184.

Note-taking is about **thinking**, not just **copying**.

A word about acknowledgement

Because you're piggy-backing on other people's work, you have to let your reader know that—to give credit where credit is due. You can do this either in the text of the essay, in footnotes or in a list of sources at the end.

Once you've found your source, you can't just lift slabs of it and plonk them into your essay. You have to transform the information by putting it into your own words and shaping it for your own purposes. An essential first step in this process is taking notes. If you can summarise a piece of information in a short note, it means you've understood it and made it your own. Later, when you write it out in a sentence, it will be your *own* sentence, organised for your *own* purposes.

How to take notes

★ Before you start taking notes, put a heading that tells you exactly what the source is. This means you can find it again quickly if you need to and you can acknowledge it. In the case of a book, you should note the name of the author, the title of the book, the date and place of publication, and the page or chapter number. The call number (the library number on the spine) is also useful. (It's tempting to skip this step, and I often have. The price is high, though—frustrating hours spent flipping through half-a-dozen books looking for one particular paragraph so you can acknowledge the source of your information or find some more detail.)

★ Use the table of contents and the index to go straight to the relevant parts.

★ Skim-read to save time once you've got to the relevant parts.

★ Write down the main words of the idea with just enough connecting words for your note to make sense.

★ Put only one point per line.

★ Sometimes turning the information into a diagram is the best way to make notes.

★ Put your notes under headings so you can see the information in bundles. Often, the research is already organised under headings: you can just copy those.

★ If you can't see how to reduce a big lump of research to a few snappy lines, try the 'MDE' trick: find its Main idea, then its Details, then any Examples.

★ Develop a shorthand that works for you—shorten words (for example, char. for character), use graphics (for example, sideways arrows to show cause and effect, up and down arrows to show things increasing or decreasing).

The cheat's note-taking

People often 'take notes' by highlighting or underlining the relevant parts of a book or article. This is certainly easier than making your own notes, but it's not nearly as useful. The moment when you work out how to summarise an idea in your own words is the moment when that idea becomes *yours*. Just running a highlighter across someone else's words doesn't do that—the idea stays in their words, in *their* brain. It hasn't been digested by you.

A bad idea: it ruins the book for the next person.

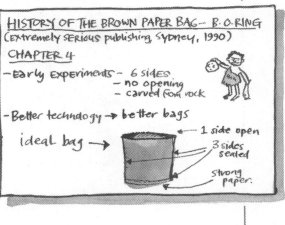

Freewriting

Freewriting is just a fancy word for talking onto the page—a way of thinking aloud about the topic in an unstructured way. It's like the 'free association' exercises that psychologists use: it's just non-stop writing.

The reason freewriting works is that you can let your brain off the leash for a while and send it out to find ideas. Ideas are shy little things and they won't come if you try to bully them, or if you keep criticising them. The important thing with freewriting is not to stop and think. Just keep the ideas flowing out the end of your pen onto the page.

It's true that your essay needs to be thought-out and planned, and it will be. But this isn't *the essay*—this is just another way of *getting ideas* for the essay. There's a time to question whether these ideas are useful. But that time isn't now. Now is the time to invite in any ideas that may happen by.

Getting ideas for an essay

Making a list

The assignment I've given myself is:

> 'Every story is a journey towards self-discovery.' Using a novel you've read this year as an example, show why you agree or disagree with this statement.

There seem to be several key words in this assignment: one is 'a novel you've read this year' and the other is 'self-discovery'. I'll take them one at a time.

I'll start by listing what I can think of about novels 'I've read this year', then list what I can think of about 'self-discovery'.

'A novel I've read this year'	'Self-discovery'
What have I read?	What exactly is self-discovery?
Tomorrow, When the War Began	How define?
Looking for Alibrandi	Discovering you can do something?
Huckleberry Finn	Learning how to do something?
The Day of the Triffids	Learning from mistakes?
	Learning about your own character?

While I was doing it, this list seemed like rubbish. But now that I look at what I've written, I can see that it tells me two things I could do next:

★ I could find out more about what 'self-discovery' means.

★ I could go back to the novels I've listed and see if there's 'self-discovery' in any of them.

A big, vague, woolly problem has turned into two quite specific smaller problems, and I can see where to go next.

Making a cluster diagram

In the middle I put the key word of my assignment. To get myself going, I'll start with a few ideas from my list. As I do this, new ideas start coming.

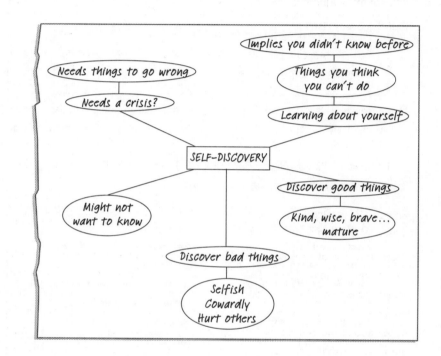

Researching

I'm going to investigate this topic by looking at four sources of information.

Research source 1: Macquarie Dictionary (1st edn), page 523

'Self-discovery' isn't in this dictionary, but 'discovery' and 'discover' are:

> Discover: To get knowledge of, learn of, or find out; gain sight or knowledge of something previously unseen or unknown.

Research source 2: Tomorrow, When the War Began by John Marsden

From the list of novels I've read this year, I choose *Tomorrow, When the War Began* by John Marsden. It's a book that shows a group of characters under pressure, and I think some of them probably go through 'self-discovery'. I read the book again with 'self-discovery' in mind and make notes about the self-discovery of the main character, Ellie. I note the page numbers so that I can easily find them again—that way, I can actually use quotes from the book when I write the essay.

> page 69—Ellie explodes mower—learns about defending herself
> 82—steps into light—learns she can be brave
> 95—thinks about having killed 3 people
> 161—thinks she's a monster
> 161—doesn't want to be 'town slut'
> 164—surprised that she recovers from guilt of killing
> 184—confused—likes both Homer and Lee
> 194—realises with Homer the attraction is only physical

Research source 3: Information about the novel

I look up a library catalogue under 'adolescent fiction' and find a book that has a chapter about John Marsden's work: *The Adolescent Novel: Australian Perspectives* by Maureen Nimon and John Foster, Centre for Information Studies, Wagga Wagga, 1997. There's a sentence or two that seem relevant to my topic.

> ...by the end of the second volume, Robyn becomes aware of a fact that the reader would have noticed already: that she and her friends have actually gained something by their involvement in the war...the characters realise how they have matured and developed...
> (page 177)

Rather than take notes here, I photocopy the extract because I might want to use it word-for-word as a quote in my essay.

Research source 4: Background information about the book

I go to John Marsden's website: www.ozemail.com.au/~andrewf/john.html

A Word from John Marsden

Lots of people have asked where the ideas for the series originated. Of course with any book there are many elements. For me, my father's stories about World War II were pretty powerful. He fought in the Middle East, Borneo and New Guinea, and was shot in the leg. I was also impressed by the attacks on Australia by the Japanese Navy and Air Force. Most people have forgotten already but Darwin was heavily bombed for a long period in 1942 and Japanese submarines, manned by brave sailors, got into Sydney Harbour, causing devastation and substantial loss of life. It seems to me that in the nineties Australians have become a bit too complacent, and no-one is seriously concerned about our security.

Another spur for writing the books was watching an Anzac Day Parade and wondering how today's teenagers would react if they were placed in the same position as their grandparents and great-grandparents in the two world wars. So many people see today's teenagers as drug-and-alcohol crazed graffiti vandals, but I was fairly sure that given a challenge the teenagers of the nineties would show as much courage and maturity as their predecessors.

Again, I might use parts of this as a quote in my essay, so I've printed the page out rather than making notes.

Freewriting

I start by quoting the topic, to give myself a run-up. Then I just keep burbling on.

nearly stopped, made myself keep writing

just keep that pen moving

slowed down, nearly gave up

`Every story is a journey towards self-discovery'—is this true? Every story seems like a big claim—does Red Riding Hood come to self-discovery? Or Cinderella? Not sure. Don't know...yes, in Tomorrow, When the War Began. Ellie discovers she's tough. So tough she kills people. What else, what else, what else? Also discovers feelings she didn't know she had—for Lee & Homer. Discovers she's confused about her feelings—she's keen on both Lee & Homer & doesn't want them to know. What else? Something about the way she feels about her parents. The roles are reversed, she has to look after them now. Feels responsible for them. Maybe that's another sort of self-discovery—sense of obligation. Obligation not coming from what her parents tell her to do but from within herself. First chapter—all the kids have to talk their parents into letting them go camping. Whereas later on they have to make their own decisions about what's right & wrong. Is that all? That seems to be all. I can't think of anything. What about the other characters in the book as well as the narrator? Does Homer go through self-discovery? Or did he always know he was a leader type—it's just that no one else knew it. Not sure about the other characters. Stick to Ellie.

From having no ideas, I've now got pages of them. Nothing earth-shattering maybe, but better than a blank page.

Getting ideas for an essay
MAKING A LIST

1 Write the assignment at the top of a page

★ If you've got an essay assignment you can use that. Or you can use my assignment. Or, you can adapt some of the assignments on pages 4–5 by inserting the title of a book or poem you've studied.

2 Work out what the assignment wants you to do

Ask yourself:

★ What's the basic subject area of this assignment?

★ What's the exact task I'm being asked to do?

> Hint…look for the **key word/s** in the assignment.

3 Start making a list

★ Write the key word as the first item on the list.

★ List anything that comes into your head about that word.

★ Use a new line for each idea.

★ Write just a word or two for each idea.

★ If there is more than one key word, list all you can about the first, then repeat the process for the second.

> Hint…look for the **task word/s** and the **limiting word/s**.

4 Can't do it?

Ask yourself:

★ Am I rejecting the ideas before I even write them down?
(Solution: don't think, just write.)

★ Am I letting the Voice of Doom bully me into stopping?
(Solution: don't try to argue with it—go on writing anyway.)

★ Am I worrying that these ideas won't work for my piece?
(Solution: don't think about *writing an essay*, just think about *writing a list*.)

★ Am I worrying that my ideas aren't on the topic?
(Solution: worry later about that. The *essay* has to be on the topic, but this *list* doesn't.)

★ Am I worrying that I'm spelling the words wrongly or not using the right ones?
(Solution: use any words you like and spell them any way you like at this stage.)

★ Am I weird because I'm finding this hard?
(Solution: no, you're like everyone else on the planet.)

> Relax...starting a piece of writing is hard for everyone.

5 When your list fills the page, you can stop and read it over

If this list doesn't look like enough, don't panic. There are lots of other ways to get ideas.

MAKING A CLUSTER DIAGRAM

1 **Make a box in the middle of the page and write the key word of the assignment in it**

★ Take your time making it look nice because while you're busy doing that, part of your brain is actually thinking about the assignment.

2 **Draw a line out from the box**

Ask yourself:

★ What does this make me think of?

3 **Write that thought down**

★ Wrap it in a little idea bubble.

★ Attach it to the box the key word is in.

4 **Keep asking questions about the key word**

★ Does it make me remember something I've read or learned about this subject?

★ Does it make me remember something that once happened to me?

★ Does it make me think of another word?

★ Does it make me think of its opposite?

★ Does it make me think of something that seems to have nothing to do with the topic?

5 **Ask questions about the idea bubbles, too**

★ Does this make me remember something else?

★ Can I extend this idea one step further? Then another step?

Hint...just put down the first thing that comes into your head.

Hint...write it down anyway—it might turn out to be useful.

Hint...a messy cluster diagram is a good cluster diagram.

6 Getting stuck?

Ask yourself:

★ Am I pre-judging my ideas?
(Solution: leave the judging of them till later.)

★ Am I worrying that I'm going off into irrelevant ideas?
(Solution: worry later about whether they're relevant.)

★ Am I getting bogged down repeating myself?
(Solution: go back to the key word, or to one of the bubbles, and start again.)

★ Is my diagram all lopsided?

Relax...lopsided is fine for a cluster diagram.

RESEARCHING

➊ Choose something from your list to find more information about

Ask yourself:

★ Is there a person, place or an event that I can find out more about?

★ Is there a general idea or concept that I can fill in with specific details?

➋ Start looking for more information

Ask yourself:

★ Is there a reference book I can look up (a dictionary, encyclopedia, atlas…)?

★ Is there a book about the subject (either non-fiction or fiction)?

★ Can I find sites about this on the Net?

★ Is there a film or video about this?

➌ Decide whether to research personally

Ask yourself:

★ Is there someone I can interview about this (either an individual or a group)?

★ Can I investigate it by observing it myself (going and having a good *look* at what I'm researching)?

★ Can I investigate it by experiencing it directly (doing it myself)?

Hint…
researching is
like fishing—the
bigger your net,
the more fish
you'll catch.

4 How to tell when you've found something useful

Ask yourself:

★ Did I find something directly useful—something that relates directly to the key word in the topic—a date, a fact, an idea?

★ Did I find something that doesn't seem directly useful, but it sticks in my mind?

★ Did I find some specific examples of something I've been thinking about in general terms? (For example, you were thinking about 'self-discovery' in a general way and now you have particular kinds of self-discovery and specific examples of it.)

★ Did I read something that someone else has said about the subject that I could use as a direct quote?

★ Did I experience or observe something that gives me a different perspective or insight?

5 Make a quick note of what you find, and where it's located

More info on note-taking can be found on page 30.

Hint...don't let the Voice of Doom talk you out of it. Write it down.

Hint...in the essay, you may not be able to use the personal experience itself, but you can use the insight that came out of it.

FREEWRITING

1 **Get some kind of timer and set it for five minutes**

★ This is so you don't have to keep checking on how many minutes you've done.

2 **Write the main words of the topic at the top of the page**

★ Keep writing without stopping.

★ If you can't think of anything else to write and you want to stop, don't.

> Keep the pen moving across the paper no matter what comes out.

3 **What if I really can't keep going?**

Ask yourself:

★ Am I trying to plan in advance what I'll say?
(Solution: let each word suggest the next one—just go forward one word at a time.)

★ Am I worried about writing something silly?
(Solution: write something *really* silly, then you can stop worrying about it. Try: 'I can't think of anything to write. This is ridiculous. This is the silliest thing I've ever done', etc. Eventually your brain will get bored with that and come up with something else.)

> Relax…this isn't the essay, it's just warming up.

★ Am I worrying about spelling and using the proper words?
(Solution: relax, you're going to fix all that in Step Six.)

★ Do I keep wanting to stop and read what I've written?
(Solution: promise yourself you can do that…but not till the timer goes off.)

★ Am I going round in circles saying the same thing over and over? (Solution: take a fresh page and give yourself a run-up with one of these writing starters:

'The thing about [key word] is...'

'I don't know much about [key word] but I do know that...'

'This isn't really relevant, but the thing that comes to mind about [key word] is...')

4 Think automatic writing

It's a Zen kind of thing—just let whatever comes, come.

Recap

From having only a blank page and no ideas, you've now got plenty of ideas, and plenty of words on paper. The next step is to choose which of those words might be useful for your piece of writing.

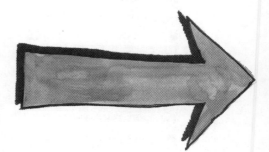

STEP TWO *Choosing*

What's in STEP TWO

About choosing ideas

This step is about having a look at all the ideas we've got and assessing them. This is where we start to discriminate between the ideas we definitely can't use, and ones that have some potential. To do that, we need to remind ourselves what our writing job is trying to do.

The purpose of imaginative writing, you'll remember, is to 'entertain', so for choosing an idea the test will be: can the idea be made **'entertaining'**? The answer will be yes if the idea could engage a reader's feelings, let the reader see or hear something, or make a reader want to know what happened next.

The purpose of an essay is to **persuade** or **inform** or both, so the test we'll use will be: can this idea be used as part of an argument, or as information about the topic? The answer will be yes if the idea would give the reader facts about the subject, a general concept about it, or an opinion about it, or if the idea could be used as supporting material or evidence.

Once you've chosen the ideas you think you can use, two things will happen:

★ You'll get a sense of the shape your piece might take—what it could be *about*.

★ You'll see where there are gaps—where you need to think up a few more ideas.

You might be thinking: 'Why didn't we just gather useful ideas in the first place?' The reason is that useful ideas and useless ideas often come together in the same bundle. If you never let the useless ideas in, you'll miss some of the useful ones too.

The next section is about imaginative writing.
If you want to go on with essay writing, skip ahead to page 57.

Choosing: auditioning your ideas, finding the stars.

To end up with ten good ideas, you need to start with twenty ordinary ones.

Choosing ideas for imaginative writing

Imaginative writing has to **entertain** your readers. That means it's got to engage their **feelings**—sadness or excitement or amusement. It can also mean you arouse their desire to know what happens next—they're caught up in a **story** or plot. Imaginative writing can't happen in a vacuum—it has to happen in a specific place to specific characters. **Descriptions** of any of these will be part of what makes the piece entertain the reader.

For imaginative writing, we can apply the following three tests to our ideas: the **feeling** test, the **story** test, and the **description** test.

1. The feeling test

★ Could I use this idea to get the reader's feelings involved to make them amused, frightened, angry, or pleased?

★ Could I use this idea to help the reader identify with this and recognise feelings from their own experience—make them think: 'Oh yes, I've felt that'?

2. The story test

★ Could I use this idea as part of an ongoing story?

★ Can I think of something that happened just before it or something that happened just after it?

★ Is it about an actual incident at a particular moment in time (rather than things in general)?

★ Could I use it to make a reader ask: 'What happened next'?

3. The description test

★ Could I use this idea as the description of a person, place or thing in the story (a place where a story might happen, a person it might happen to, or a thing that could be significant)?

★ Could I use it to create a mood or atmosphere?

★ Could I use it to help a reader actually *see* what's happening?

There's a difference between writing **about** feelings and actually **creating feelings** in readers. You can use a word like 'embarrassing' *about* a feeling, but it won't **make the feeling happen** in a reader.

Any **event** can be part of a **story**.

If you can draw a picture of it, it passes the test.

Choosing ideas for imaginative writing

Choosing from the list

In Step One I said that my imaginative writing assignment is: *Write a piece with the title 'Steep Learning Curve'*. Here's the list I made in Step One. I'll go through and see which ideas pass one of the three tests.

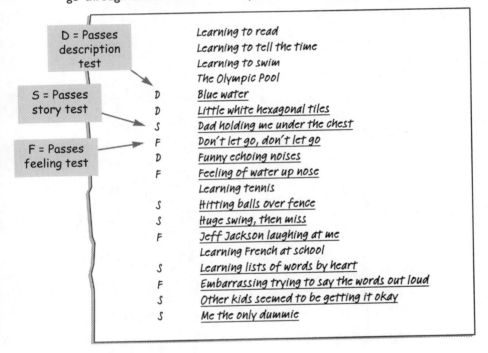

> **D = Passes description test**
>
> **S = Passes story test**
>
> **F = Passes feeling test**

	Learning to read
	Learning to tell the time
	Learning to swim
	The Olympic Pool
D	Blue water
D	Little white hexagonal tiles
S	Dad holding me under the chest
F	Don't let go, don't let go
D	Funny echoing noises
F	Feeling of water up nose
	Learning tennis
S	Hitting balls over fence
S	Huge swing, then miss
F	Jeff Jackson laughing at me
	Learning French at school
S	Learning lists of words by heart
F	Embarrassing trying to say the words out loud
S	Other kids seemed to be getting it okay
S	Me the only dummie

Choosing from the cluster diagram

Here's my cluster diagram from Step One.

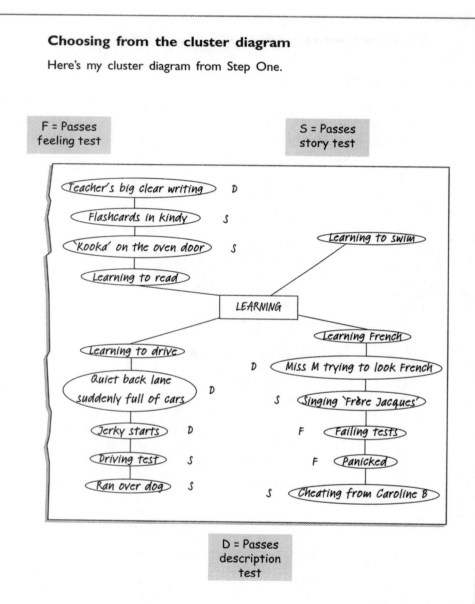

F = Passes feeling test

S = Passes story test

Teacher's big clear writing — D

Flashcards in kindy — S

'Kooka' on the oven door — S

Learning to read

Learning to swim

LEARNING

Learning French

Learning to drive

D — Miss M trying to look French

Quiet back lane suddenly full of cars — D

S — Singing 'Frère Jacques'

Jerky starts — D

F — Failing tests

Driving test — S

F — Panicked

Ran over dog — S

S — Cheating from Caroline B

D = Passes description test

Choosing from research

First, here is my **idea-getting research** from Step One, and the notes I did from it.

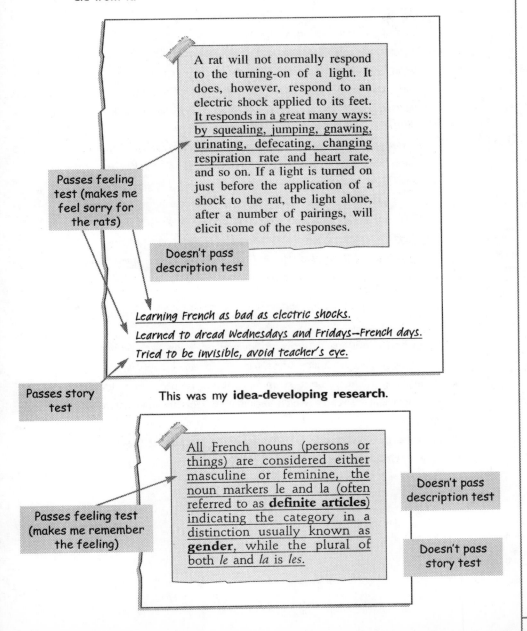

A rat will not normally respond to the turning-on of a light. It does, however, respond to an electric shock applied to its feet. It responds in a great many ways: by squealing, jumping, gnawing, urinating, defecating, changing respiration rate and heart rate, and so on. If a light is turned on just before the application of a shock to the rat, the light alone, after a number of pairings, will elicit some of the responses.

Passes feeling test (makes me feel sorry for the rats)

Doesn't pass description test

Learning French as bad as electric shocks.

Learned to dread Wednesdays and Fridays—French days.

Tried to be invisible, avoid teacher's eye.

Passes story test

This was my **idea-developing research**.

All French nouns (persons or things) are considered either masculine or feminine, the noun markers le and la (often referred to as **definite articles**) indicating the category in a distinction usually known as **gender**, while the plural of both *le* and *la* is *les.*

Passes feeling test (makes me remember the feeling)

Doesn't pass description test

Doesn't pass story test

Choosing from freewriting

Here's the freewriting I did in Step One.

> Learning—hard and embarrassing, you can't do it, you feel
> stupid. Worse with people who already know how to do it. Now
> what? I can't think of anything else to write. I don't think
> this is working French was the worst, it didn't make sense.
> Maison meant house, I could learn that, a bit like mansion.
> But what about the 'le' and 'la' business? How were you
> supposed to remember that—two different words for 'the'?
> Why? Why some 'feminine' and some 'masculine'? I asked Miss
> M—Why is 'leg' feminine and 'foot' masculine. She gave me
> that 'what a dummie' look. The whole class staring at me. Now
> I've run out of things to I cheated. Copied from Caroline B
> next to me. She tried to stop me, sloped her page away and
> hid it behind her hand. Maybe I really wanted to be found
> cheating, so someone would rescue me.

Passes feeling test

Passes story test

Passes feeling test

From having nothing to write about and no ideas at the start of Step One, I've now got too many ideas for one piece. I could write a piece about learning French, about swimming, about tennis, about learning to drive or learning to read...which should I use for my imaginative writing piece?

I'll make that decision in Step Three, when I'm putting these ideas into an outline. First, you try choosing.

Choosing ideas for imaginative writing
FROM THE LIST YOU MADE IN STEP ONE

1 Apply the feeling test to it

Ask yourself:
* Is this about a feeling?
* Does it make me *feel* a feeling?
* Would others be likely to recognise this feeling?

If the answer to any of these is yes, choose it. (Use a highlighter or just draw a circle around it.)

> Hint ... would most people think, 'Oh yes, I've felt that'?

2 Apply the story test to it

Ask yourself:
* Could I use this as part of a story?
* Could I think of what might have gone before it or what might happen after it?
* Is this about an actual incident involving a particular person, at a particular time, in a particular place?
* Could this start: 'One day...'?
* Could I use this to make a reader think: 'And what happened after that'?

If the answer to any of these is yes, choose it.

> Hint ... good stories can grow from tiny unimpressive seeds.

3 Apply the description test to it

Ask yourself:
* Could this describe a place in my piece of writing?
* Could this describe a person?
* Could this describe an object?
* Does this help a reader see or hear?
* Could this help to create a mood or atmosphere?

If the answer to any of these is yes, choose it.

4 What if this isn't working?

Ask yourself:

★ Am I setting my standards for choosing unrealistically high?
(Solution: lower them—just to get yourself started—even Shakespeare had to start somewhere.)

★ Am I trying to find things that could be used just as they are?
(Solution: recognise that these early ideas might have to be changed before you can use them.)

★ Am I disappointed not to be choosing more ideas?
(Solution: even if you only choose a couple of ideas from your list that's okay. You can build on them.)

> Relax…you're auditioning for potential here, not a polished performance.

5 Repeat this process with the other things you did in Step One

★ the cluster diagram;

★ the research;

★ the freewriting.

What you have now is a collection of ideas with potential to be used in your piece.

The next section is about essay writing. If you want to go on with imaginative writing, skip ahead to Step Three (page 67).

Choosing ideas for an essay

The purpose of an essay, you'll remember, is to **persuade** or **inform** or both. That means engaging the readers' thoughts rather than their feelings.

They might get some **information** from your essay or they might see information arranged to illustrate a general **concept**. Or they might be persuaded of a particular point of view about the topic. In this case the point of view will be supported by examples and other kinds of **evidence**.

For an essay, then, we'll apply the following three basic tests to all our ideas:

1. The information test

★ Does this idea provide any facts about the subject (for example, a definition, a date, a statistic or background information)?

2. The concept test

★ Could I use this to put forward a general concept about a subject (an opinion, a general truth or a summary)?

★ Could I use this as part of a theory or an opinion about the subject (either my own or someone else's)?

3. The evidence test

★ Could I use this to support any information I present?

★ Could I use this to support an opinion (point of view) or theory about the subject?

★ Is it a concrete example of the idea I'm putting forward?

★ Is it a quote from an authority on the subject, or some other kind of supporting material?

At this stage you probably don't know exactly what arguments or points your essay is going to make. That's okay, you don't have to know that yet. Going through the ideas you have and applying these tests will help you clarify that.

Now, I'm going to go through all the bits I wrote in Step One and choose anything that will pass any of these three tests.

A good essay needs all three of these.

Chicken and egg again...let the **ideas** come first and suggest the **theme**.

Choosing ideas for an essay

Choosing from my list

First, I'll remind myself of what my topic is: *'Every story is a journey towards self-discovery.' Using a novel you've read this year as an example, show why you agree or disagree with this statement.*

Here's the list I made in Step One. I'll go through and see which ideas pass any of the tests for an essay.

Doesn't pass concept test

Passes evidence test (when I've chosen one)

'A novel I've read this year'
What have I read?
Tomorrow, When the War Began
Looking for Alibrandi
Huckleberry Finn
The Day of the Triffids

'Self-discovery'
What exactly is self-discovery?
How define?
Discovering you can do something?
Learning how to do something?
Learning from mistakes?
Learning about your own character?

Passes information test (or it will, when I have this information)

Choosing from the cluster diagram

Here's my cluster diagram from Step One.

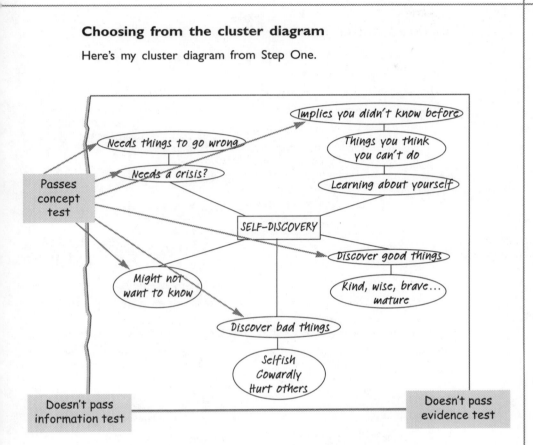

Choosing from research

The first piece of research from Step One I've got is the dictionary definition of 'discovery'. It passes just one of the tests.

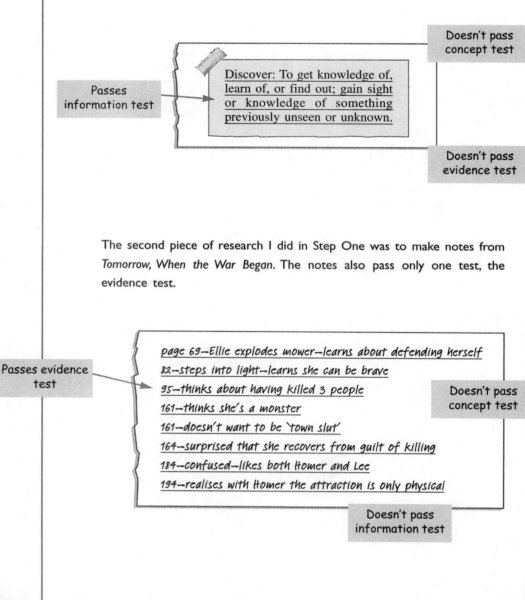

Doesn't pass concept test

Passes information test

Discover: To get knowledge of, learn of, or find out; gain sight or knowledge of something previously unseen or unknown.

Doesn't pass evidence test

The second piece of research I did in Step One was to make notes from *Tomorrow, When the War Began*. The notes also pass only one test, the evidence test.

Passes evidence test

page 69—Ellie explodes mower—learns about defending herself
82—steps into light—learns she can be brave
95—thinks about having killed 3 people
161—thinks she's a monster
161—doesn't want to be 'town slut'
164—surprised that she recovers from guilt of killing
184—confused—likes both Homer and Lee
194—realises with Homer the attraction is only physical

Doesn't pass concept test

Doesn't pass information test

My third research source in Step One was the book *The Adolescent Novel.*

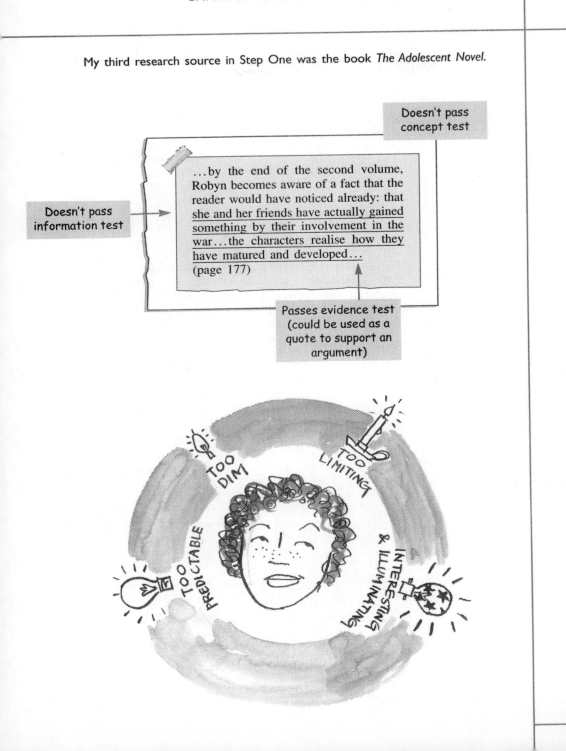

Doesn't pass concept test

Doesn't pass information test

...by the end of the second volume, Robyn becomes aware of a fact that the reader would have noticed already: that she and her friends have actually gained something by their involvement in the war...the characters realise how they have matured and developed...
(page 177)

Passes evidence test (could be used as a quote to support an argument)

TOO DIM

TOO LIMITING

TOO PREDICTABLE

INTERESTING & ILLUMINATING

The fourth piece of research was the extract from John Marsden's website.

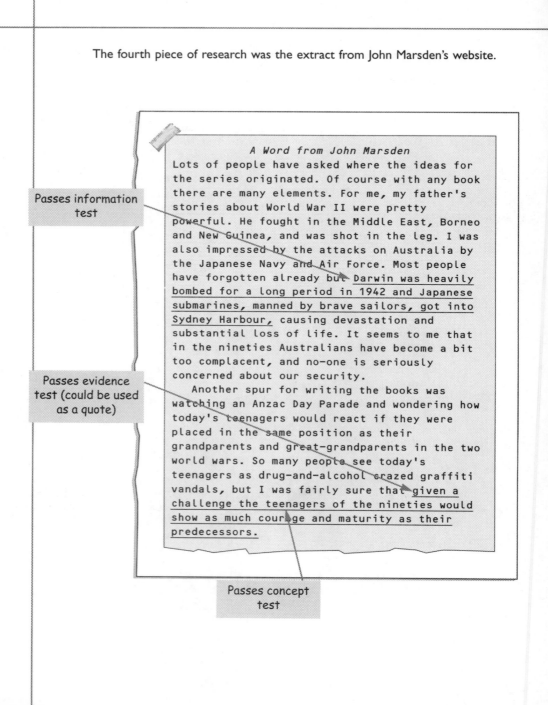

Passes information test

Passes evidence test (could be used as a quote)

Passes concept test

A Word from John Marsden
Lots of people have asked where the ideas for the series originated. Of course with any book there are many elements. For me, my father's stories about World War II were pretty powerful. He fought in the Middle East, Borneo and New Guinea, and was shot in the leg. I was also impressed by the attacks on Australia by the Japanese Navy and Air Force. Most people have forgotten already but Darwin was heavily bombed for a long period in 1942 and Japanese submarines, manned by brave sailors, got into Sydney Harbour, causing devastation and substantial loss of life. It seems to me that in the nineties Australians have become a bit too complacent, and no-one is seriously concerned about our security.

Another spur for writing the books was watching an Anzac Day Parade and wondering how today's teenagers would react if they were placed in the same position as their grandparents and great-grandparents in the two world wars. So many people see today's teenagers as drug-and-alcohol crazed graffiti vandals, but I was fairly sure that given a challenge the teenagers of the nineties would show as much courage and maturity as their predecessors.

Choosing from freewriting

Here's the piece of freewriting I did in Step One.

`Every story is a journey towards self-discovery'—is this true?
Every story seems like a big claim—does Red Riding Hood come
to self-discovery? Or Cinderella? Not sure. Dont' know...yes, in
Tomorrow, When the War Began. Ellie discovers she's tough. So
tough she kills people. What else, what else, what else? Also
discovers feelings she didn't know she had—for Lee & Homer.
Discovers she's confused about her feelings—she's keen on both
Lee & Homer & doesn't want them to know. What else?
Something about the way she feels about her parents. The roles
are reversed, she has to look after them now. Feels responsible
for them. Maybe that's another sort of self-discovery—sense of
obligation. Obligation not coming from what her parents tell her
to do but from within herself. First chapter—all the kids have
to talk their parents into letting them go camping. Whereas
later on they have to make their own decisions about what's
right & wrong. Is that all? That seems to be all. I can't think
of anything. What about the other characters in the book as well
as the narrator? Does Homer go through self-discovery? Or did
he always know he was a leader type—it's just that no one else
knew it. Not sure about the other characters. Stick to Ellie.

Passes evidence test

Passes concept test

Doesn't pass information test

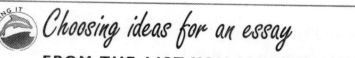

Choosing ideas for an essay

FROM THE LIST YOU MADE IN STEP ONE

1 Apply the information test to it

Ask yourself:

★ Could I use this to clarify the terms of the assignment (a definition, explanation of words)?

★ Could I use this to clarify the limitations of the assignment (narrowing it to a particular aspect)?

★ Could I use this as a fact (a date, a name, a statistic)?

★ Could I use this as general background information (historical overview, some sort of 'the story so far…')?

If the answer to any of these is yes, choose it.

2 Apply the concept test to it

Ask yourself:

★ Could I use this as part of a general concept about the subject (a general truth or broad idea)?

★ Is this an opinion about the subject (either my own or someone else's)?

★ Could I use this as part of a theory about the subject?

If the answer to any of these is yes, choose it.

3 **Apply the evidence test to it**

Ask yourself:

★ Could I use this as an example of something to do with the assignment?

★ Could I use this to support any idea or point of view about the assignment?

★ Is this a quote from an authority or an established fact, or any kind of specific case in point?

If the answer to any of these is yes, choose it.

Hint...you might need some imagination to see how to use ideas.

4 **What if this isn't working?**

Ask yourself:

★ Am I stuck because I'm not sure exactly what points I'll make in my essay?
(Solution: you don't have to know that yet. Just choose anything that seems relevant to the assignment. Once you've chosen your ideas, then you can work out exactly how to use them.)

★ Am I setting my standards for choosing unrealistically high?
(Solution: lower them, just to get yourself started—even Einstein had to start somewhere.)

★ Am I trying to find things that could be used just as they are?
(Solution: recognise that these early ideas might have to be changed before you can use them.)

★ Am I disappointed not to be choosing more ideas?
(Solution: even if you only choose a couple of ideas from your list, that's okay. You can build on them.)

Relax...you're auditioning for potential here, not a polished performance.

5 **Repeat this process with the other things you did in Step One**

★ the cluster diagram;

★ the research;

★ the freewriting.

Recap

What you have now is a collection of ideas that are all within the broad outlines of your assignment. Next, you'll make some decisions about how to use these ideas.

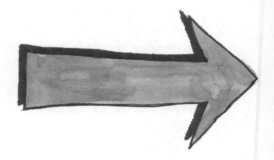

STEP THREE
Outlining

Putting your ideas in the Best ORDER...

What's in STEP THREE

About making an outline

An outline is a working plan for a piece of writing. It's a list of all the ideas that are going to be in the piece in the order they should go. Once you've got the outline planned, you can stop worrying about the structure and just concentrate on getting each sentence right.

In order to make an outline, you need to know basically what you're going to say in your piece—in other words, what your *theme* is.

An outline is also known as:
* a map
* a flowchart
* a plan.

Themes

One way to find a theme is to think one up out of thin air, and then make all your ideas fit around it. Another way is to let the ideas point you to the theme—you *follow* your ideas, rather than *direct* them.

As you do this, you'll find that your ideas aren't as haphazard as you thought. Some will turn out to be about the same thing. Some can be put into a sequence. Some might pair off into opposing groups. Out of these natural groupings, your theme will gradually emerge. This way, your theme is not just an abstract concept in a vacuum, which you need to then prop up with enough ideas to fill a few pages. Instead, your theme comes with all its supporting ideas automatically attached.

Using index cards

One of the easiest ways to let your ideas form into patterns is to separate them, so you can physically shuffle them around. Writing each idea on a separate card or slip of paper can allow you to see connections between them that you'd never see otherwise.

Making an outline involves trial and error—but it only takes seconds to move cards into a new outline. If you try to start writing before the outline works properly, it could take you all week to rewrite and rewrite again.

In an exam, you can't use cards (see page 208 for another way to do it), and you'll gradually develop a way that suits you. But doing an outline on cards—even a few times—can show you just how easy it is to rearrange your ideas.

Finding the patterns in your ideas

One way to put your ideas into order so that your theme can emerge is to use the most basic kind of order, shared by all kinds of writing:

1. **A Beginning**—some kind of introduction, telling the reader where they are and what kind of thing they're about to read.

2. **A Middle**—the main bit, where you say what you're there to say.

3. **An End**—some kind of winding-up part that lets the reader know that this is actually the end of the piece (rather than that someone lost the last page).

Exactly what's inside the compartments of Beginning, Middle and End of a piece of writing depends on whether it's a piece of imaginative writing, an essay or some other kind of writing. It helps to remember that behind their differences, all writing shares the same three-part structure—just as all hamburgers do.

Obvious, but then so is a lifeboat!

TOP BUN
Where it all starts: a beginning that
gives the reader something to bite into

FILLING
A middle that gives the reader all kinds
of different stuff

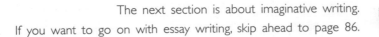

BOTTOM BUN
Finishing off the piece: something to
hold it all together

The next section is about imaginative writing.
If you want to go on with essay writing, skip ahead to page 86.

Making an outline for imaginative writing

Like all writing, imaginative writing can be reduced to the three basic parts: **Beginning**, **Middle** and **End**. Sort your ideas into these groups and you'll soon see what your piece will be about. If you summarise each idea on a card, this process will be much easier.

Beginning

For imaginative writing, this is often called the **orientation** (working out where you are). It is where the scene is set and the characters are introduced. Beginnings might include:

★ a description (of characters, settings or objects);

★ essential information (to place the reader in time and space);

★ background information (to fill in some essential past information).

Middle

For imaginative writing, this is sometimes called the **complication**—where the initial situation is complicated by some new factor. It's where the action gets going, and we see how the characters respond. A Middle might include:

★ an incident that sets off a chain of cause and effect;

★ character development;

★ a response by the characters to what's happening;

★ a revealing of how the characters feel about what's happening ('evaluation');

★ dialogue.

'Once upon a time there was...'

'Suddenly...'

IMAGINATIVE WRITING

End

This is often called the **resolution** in imaginative writing. It's where the complicating factor is resolved or defused in some way. An End might include:

★ a punch-line or sudden reversal;

★ a surprise twist;

★ a drawing-together of different story threads;

★ a broadening-out effect, pulling back from close-ups of characters and action;

★ a focus on an image that resonates with the meaning of the piece.

Look at any book or film that works and you'll probably find it's got this fundamental three-part structure.

BEGINNING (orientation): the situation everything starts with

MIDDLE (complication): the meaty part of the story—the main drama

END (resolution): the bit that ties the story together and keeps it from falling to pieces

So the first step in creating an outline is to decide whether each idea belongs in the Beginning, the Middle, or the End.

'...and then they lived happily ever after.'

Hamburgers are simpler than writing...

A plan is a guide, not a police officer.

The problem with this neat and tidy theory is that sometimes the top bun and the bottom bun look the same. Sometimes they even look like a filling. Your bundle of ideas may not divide neatly into these three categories.

Also, a story (unlike a hamburger) is often more interesting if the order of the three steps is changed around. For example, a story can leap straight into the complication right at the beginning ('He was lying at the foot of the stairs. He was dead all right...') and then go back and do all the introductions ('I'd known him for years, a small man with a head like an egg...'). Also, you may want to get several time frames going at once (for example, using a flashback).

This is where index cards come in. They make it easy to keep on rearranging your ideas until you're happy with the order. And if you need to add some new ideas, you can just make more cards.

With imaginative writing, the best things sometimes come to you as you *write*, rather than as you *plan*. You should feel free to make changes if you think of something better, but you need a plan to get you started.

As you play around rearranging the cards, you'll probably start to see the 'big picture' of your piece—the overall shape of the story, the theme. Once you've got that, you can make a one-sentence summary of it to act as a reminder of the piece as a whole.

Making an outline for imaginative writing

First, I'll remind myself again of my assignment: *Write a piece with the title 'Steep Learning Curve'.*

Looking at the ideas I've chosen

The ideas I've got so far (from my list, my cluster diagram, my research and my freewriting) are mainly about four different learning experiences:

> *learning French;*
> *learning to swim;*
> *learning to drive;*
> *learning tennis.*

It looks as though I could have a story about any one of these, so my first job is to choose one. Glancing back over the ideas in Step One, I see that there seem to be more ideas about learning French than the other areas, and my memories about it are quite vivid. For the moment I'll decide that my story is going to be about learning French. (If this idea doesn't work out as I go along, I can always come back to one of the others.)

Index cards

I'm going to make a card for each idea I've chosen that has to do with French. The card will have just a brief summary of the idea. These are the cards I end up with:

From the list

Saying French words embarrassing

Learning off by heart

Other kids okay, me the dummie

From the cluster diagram

Miss M trying to look French

Failing French tests

Cheating

Singing 'Frère Jacques'

From research

French classes—like rats

Quote from textbook

From freewriting

'Le' and 'la' problem

Miss M unhelpful

Caroline not letting me cheat

Did I want to be caught?

Sorting the cards

The next thing is to sort the cards into the three basic categories: **Beginning**, **Middle** and **End**.

A card that belongs at the **Beginning** will help set the scene. It introduces the characters, describes the setting, or generally tells the reader where they are and what's happening. They tend to be cards that describe 'general' things that *often* happen, not particular events.

My scene is an uninspired learner in a high school French class, so I'll pick out any card that could help to orient the reader in that kind of scene.

Saying French words embarrassing

Learning off by heart

Other kids okay, me the dummie

Miss M trying to look French

Failing French tests

French classes—like rats

Quote from textbook

A card that belongs in the **Middle** introduces a **complication**—something starts *happening* at this point in the story. These cards suggest an event that could happen—one particular incident or problem.

`Le´ and `la´ problem

Singing `Frère Jacques´

Cheating

Miss M unhelpful

Caroline not letting me cheat

Did I want to be caught?

A card that belongs at the **End** shows the problem getting **resolved**, or gives a sense of winding up. I don't seem to have anything like that.

Refining the outline

Next, I rearrange the cards within each of these piles until they're in the order that seems best. (I also drop 'Frère Jacques'—it doesn't fit.)

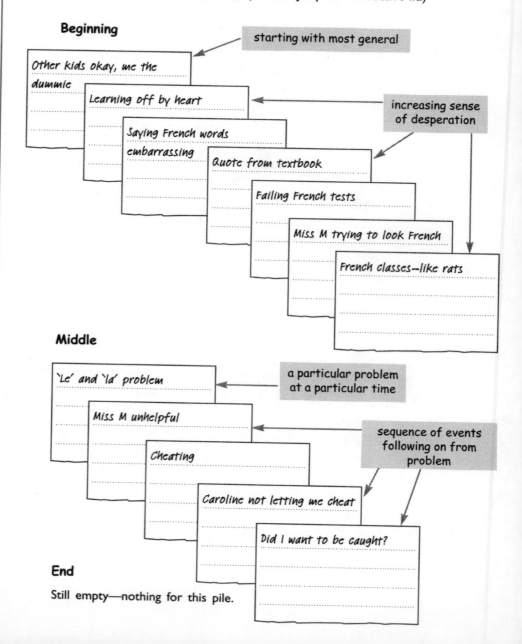

Beginning

starting with most general

Other kids okay, me the dummie

Learning off by heart

increasing sense of desperation

Saying French words embarrassing

Quote from textbook

Failing French tests

Miss M trying to look French

French classes—like rats

Middle

'Le' and 'la' problem

a particular problem at a particular time

Miss M unhelpful

sequence of events following on from problem

Cheating

Caroline not letting me cheat

Did I want to be caught?

End

Still empty—nothing for this pile.

Adding to the outline

Seeing this on cards makes it painfully obvious that I've got a very unbalanced story—there's plenty of scene-setting, a little bit of complication and no resolution at all.

I'll make two new cards for the Middle:

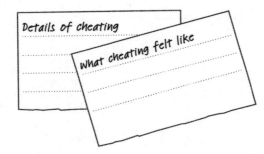

Details of cheating

What cheating felt like

I need some more ideas for an End, so I'll make a list of all the different endings I can think of.

- I'm caught cheating—sent to principal—expelled.
- I'm not caught, but feel guilty—confess and feel relieved.
- I'm not caught, but other girl's answers are wrong too.

None of these seems very good, but the last one seems the most interesting, so I'll make a new card for that.

I start to see the overall shape of the story now, so I'll make a new card with a summary of the whole piece:

Think I'm the only
dummie—cheat—other
girl's answers wrong too.

My final outline, including the new cards, looks like this:

Think I'm the only dummie
—cheat—other girl's answers
wrong too.

Beginning

Other kids okay, me the dummie

Learning off by heart

Saying French words embarrassing

Quote from textbook

Failing French tests

Miss M trying to look French

French classes—like rats

Middle

'Le' and 'la' problem

Miss M unhelpful

Cheating

How I cheated

What cheating felt like

Caroline not letting me cheat

Did I want to be caught?

End

Other girl's answers wrong too

Making an outline for imaginative writing

1 Look at the assignment again

★ This is so you don't stray off it.

2 One story or several?

★ If you've got ideas that point towards more than one story, decide which one you'll go with.

Hint...pick the one you'd **prefer** to write, not the one you think you **should** write.

3 Get some cards

★ Normal sized index cards cut in half work well.

★ Write each idea on a separate card.

★ Just a word or two will do for each (enough to remind you what the idea is).

4 Pick out cards for a Beginning pile

Ask yourself whether these cards could set the scene:

★ Could I use it to describe a person, place or thing in the story?

★ Does it establish a situation?

★ Does it introduce a character?

★ Does it feel like a 'wide shot' or a 'title squence'?

If the answer to any of these is yes, put those cards together.

Hint...some cards could work equally well in more than one place—try both.

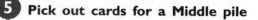

5 Pick out cards for a Middle pile

Ask yourself whether these cards could show an event happening at a particular time or place:

★ Does it introduce a new factor into the situation?

★ Does it show a problem or a conflict happening?

★ Would it make a reader wonder, 'And then what happened?'

★ Does it show characters interacting with each other (through dialogue or action)?

★ Does it show characters responding to the problem/conflict (by doing something, thinking something or feeling something)?

★ Could it be the climax—the most dramatic moment?

★ Does it feel like a 'close-up'?

If the answer to any of these is yes, put those cards together in a second pile.

6 Pick out cards for an End pile

Ask yourself whether these cards could show some kind of resolution:

★ Is a problem sidestepped or moved on from?

★ Could this be used to show a moment of equilibrium or stillness (a strong image, perhaps)?

★ Does it feel like a 'zoom out' or an 'end title sequence'?

If the answer to any of these is yes, put those cards together in a third pile.

> Hint...you may not have any cards for this pile yet.

7 Refine the outline

Ask yourself:

★ Are the cards in the Beginning in the best order?

★ Are the cards in the Middle in the best order?

★ Are the cards in the End in the best order?

8 Adding to the outline

Ask yourself:

★ Have I got big gaps that are making it hard to see an overall shape? (Solution: make temporary cards that approximately fill the gap—'describe Fred' or 'show Fred's feelings' or 'crisis'.)

★ Have I got plenty in one pile but nothing in another? (Solution: start with the pile you have most cards for. Get it in order. Then work on the other piles, making new temporary cards as you go.)

9 Not working?

★ Am I stuck because I can't think of an ending or an opening? (Solution: you don't need to know *exactly* how your piece will begin and end. Getting the middle right is the main thing—that will help you see how to begin and end.)

★ Am I trying to force in something that's so wonderful I can't bear not to use it? (Solution: put the wonderful thing in a folder called 'Good ideas to use some other time'.)

What you have now is a clear idea of what your piece is about, who's in it and where it happens. This outline will be like a map to follow when you start writing.

The next section is about essay writing. If you want to go on with imaginative writing, skip ahead to Step Four (page 103).

Hint...the climax should usually be at the end of the Middle.

Hint...this plan may change as you write—just get it roughly right.

Making an outline for an essay

You've now got a collection of ideas that all relate in some way to your essay assignment. What you'll do here is rearrange those ideas so they end up as an orderly sequence that will **inform** or **persuade** the reader.

To do that, you'll need to know what your *theme* is—the underlying argument or point of your essay. The first step towards this is to put each of your ideas on a separate card or slip of paper. That makes it much easier to find patterns in your ideas. As you look at the ideas on the cards, chances are you'll start to notice that:

★ some ideas go together, saying similar things;

★ some ideas contradict each other;

★ some ideas can be arranged into a sequence, each idea emerging out of the one before it.

By looking at these groupings, you'll begin to see how you can apply your ideas to the task of your assignment.

Once you have a basic approach (you don't need to know it in detail), you can begin to shape your ideas into an outline. Start with the most basic shape, using the fact that every piece of writing has a **Beginning**, a **Middle** and an **End**.

Beginning

Often called the **introduction**. Readers need all the help that writers can give them, so the introduction is where we tell them, briefly, what the essay will be about. Different essays need different kinds of introductions, but every introduction should have a 'thesis statement': a one-sentence statement of your basic idea. As well, an introduction may have one or more of these:

★ an **overview** of the whole subject;

★ **background** to the particular issue you're going to write about;

Sometimes you know your theme from the beginning.

Other times, your collection of ideas will tell you what the theme should be.

Tell the reader what you're going to say...

★ a **definition** or clarification of the main terms of the assignment;

★ an outline of the **different points of view** that can be taken about the assignment;

★ an outline of the **particular point of view** you plan to take in the essay.

Middle

Often called the **development**. This is where you develop, paragraph by paragraph, the points you want to make. A development might include:

★ information—facts, figures, dates, data;

★ examples—of whatever points you're making;

★ supporting material for your points—quotes, logical cause-and-effect workings, putting an idea into a larger context.

End

Often called the **conclusion**. You've said everything you want to say, but by this time your readers are in danger of forgetting where they were going in the first place, so you remind them. A conclusion might include:

★ a recap of your main points, to jog the readers' memories;

★ a summing-up that points out the larger significance or meaning of the main points;

★ a powerful image or quote that sums up the points you've been making.

Say what you're going to say...

And finally, tell the reader what you've just said.

TOP BUN
Beginning (introduction): where you tell the reader briefly how you're going to approach the subject

FILLING
Middle (development): where you lay out all the points you want to make

BOTTOM BUN
End (conclusion): this ties the essay together and relates all the bits to each other

Just sitting and looking at a list of ideas and trying to think about them in your head doesn't usually get you anywhere. Writing is like learning to play tennis—you don't learn tennis by *thinking about it*, but by *trying to do it*. You might have to spend a while rearranging your index cards—but it will save time and pain in the long run.

Different ways of organising the middle of an essay

The **Middle** of an essay should be arranged in an orderly way: you can't just throw all the bits in and hope for the best. What that 'orderly way' is, depends on your assignment.

One-pronged essays

Some assignments only ask about one kind of thing or one way of looking at a subject. In that case you can just put the filling into the burger in whatever orderly way seems best for the subject.

One kind of arrangement might be to present the ideas from the most important to least important, or from the most distant in time to the most recent.

Finding a sequence for your ideas...

INTRODUCTION

POINT 1 ABOUT ORANGES + EVIDENCE

POINT 2 ABOUT ORANGES + EVIDENCE

POINT 3 ABOUT ORANGES + EVIDENCE

CONCLUSION

Two-pronged essays

Some essays want you to deal with two subjects (not just oranges, but oranges *and* apples) or two different points of view (for example, an assignment that asks you to 'discuss' by putting the case **for** and **against** something, or an assignment that asks you to 'compare' or 'contrast' different views). With these two-pronged assignments, it's easy to get into a muddle with structure.

For two-pronged assignments you can organise the middle in either of the following ways (but not a combination!).

All the points about oranges, then all the points about apples:

INTRODUCTION

POINT 1 ABOUT ORANGES

POINT 2 ABOUT ORANGES

POINT 3 ABOUT ORANGES

POINT 1 ABOUT APPLES

POINT 2 ABOUT APPLES

POINT 3 ABOUT APPLES

CONCLUSION

One point about apples, then one point about oranges, and so on:

INTRODUCTION

POINT 1 ABOUT ORANGES

POINT 1 ABOUT APPLES

POINT 2 ABOUT ORANGES

POINT 2 ABOUT APPLES

POINT 3 ABOUT ORANGES

POINT 3 ABOUT APPLES

CONCLUSION

Making an outline for an essay

First a reminder of the assignment: '*Every story is a journey towards self-discovery.*' *Using a novel you've read this year as an example, show why you agree or disagree with this statement.*

Index cards

I'll start by making these index card summaries for the ideas I chose in Step Two:

From the list

TWTWB (*Tomorrow, When the War Began*) is a good example of the statement

What 'self-discovery' (s-d) means

From the cluster diagram

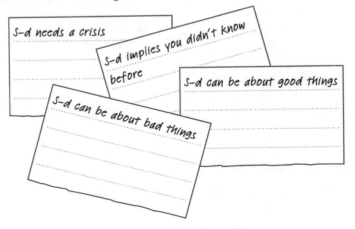

S-d needs a crisis

S-d implies you didn't know before

S-d can be about good things

S-d can be about bad things

From research

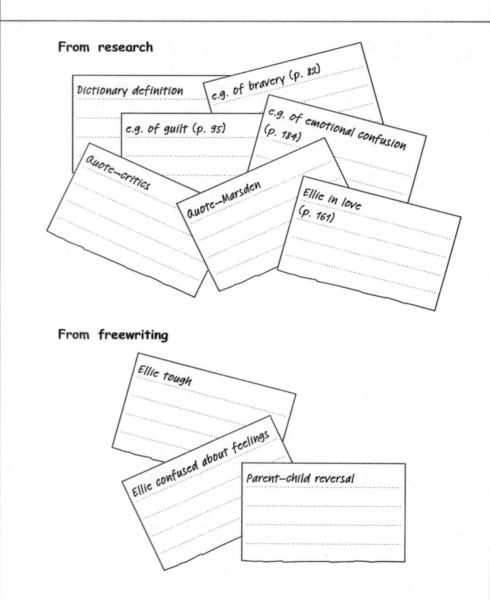

Dictionary definition

e.g. of bravery (p. 82)

e.g. of guilt (p. 95)

e.g. of emotional confusion (p. 184)

Quote—critics

Quote—Marsden

Ellie in love (p. 161)

From freewriting

Ellie tough

Ellie confused about feelings

Parent—child reversal

What groups of ideas are here?

Looking at my ideas on cards from Step Two, I can see that they fall into three main groups:

> ★ ideas about what 'self-discovery' can mean (for example, discovering good things/discovering bad things);

★ examples of Ellie's self-discovery in the novel;

★ other people's ideas (quotes from the critics and John Marsden).

Now I need to decide on my basic approach to the assignment:

★ Will I agree or disagree with the statement about self-discovery?

★ Can I support either point of view with evidence?

I decide to agree with the statement because I've got plenty of examples of self-discovery in the novel. That will do for the moment as my 'theme'.

Sorting the cards

The next thing is to sort the cards into three piles: Beginning, Middle and End.

Beginning

Cards in this pile will be any that give an introduction to the subject: an overview, background information, clarification of terms used, or general concepts about the subject.

I'll pull out all the cards that seem to do any of those things.

TWTWB a good example

What 'self-discovery' means

S-d needs a crisis

S-d implies you didn't know before

S-d can be about good things

S-d can be about bad things

Dictionary definition

Middle

Cards in this pile will develop the concepts in more detail using examples and evidence.

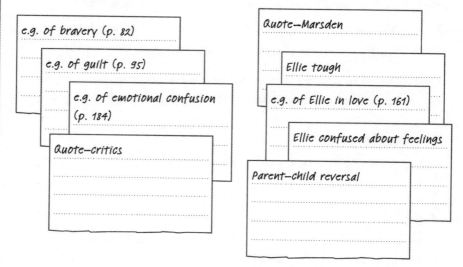

e.g. of bravery (p. 82)

e.g. of guilt (p. 95)

e.g. of emotional confusion (p. 184)

Quote—critics

Quote—Marsden

Ellie tough

e.g. of Ellie in love (p. 161)

Ellie confused about feelings

Parent—child reversal

End

Cards in this pile will draw general conclusions from the other ideas or sum them up in some way. I don't think I have any like that yet.

Refining the outline

I'll put the cards within each of these groups into the order that seems best.

Beginning

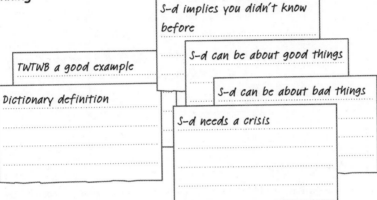

S-d implies you didn't know before

S-d can be about good things

TWTWB a good example

S-d can be about bad things

Dictionary definition

S-d needs a crisis

Middle

Looking at the cards, a natural structure suggests itself: I sort the cards into 'good kinds of self-discovery' and 'bad kinds of self-discovery'. While I was doing this, I removed a few cards that doubled up on the same idea.

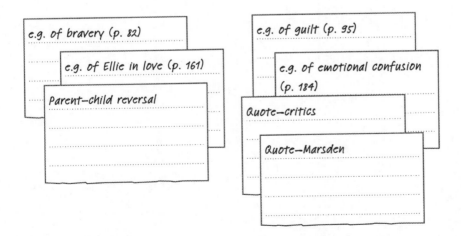

e.g. of bravery (p. 82)

e.g. of Ellie in love (p. 161)

Parent–child reversal

e.g. of guilt (p. 95)

e.g. of emotional confusion (p. 184)

Quote–critics

Quote–Marsden

All this rearranging of the cards has enabled me to see the theme more clearly. I'll make a summary card that outlines my basic argument. This will become my 'thesis statement' when I start to write the essay.

> Summary: Agree with
> statement: TWTWB a journey
> towards self-discovery—both
> good things and bad

Adding to the outline

The Beginning and the Middle seem to have enough material; however the End is blank. Just to complete the outline, I do an 'End' card even though it's almost the same as the 'theme' card.

> TWTWB—shows journey to
> self-discovery

Here's my final outline:

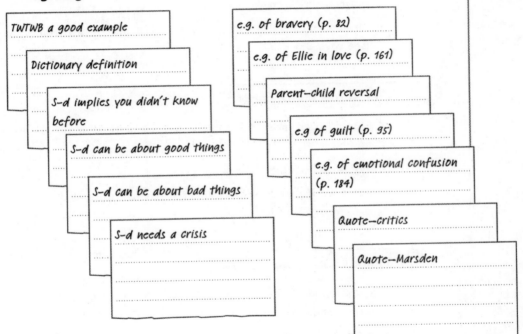

Summary: Agree with statement: TWTWB a journey towards self-discovery—both good things and bad

Beginning

TWTWB a good example

Dictionary definition

S-d implies you didn't know before

S-d can be about good things

S-d can be about bad things

S-d needs a crisis

Middle

e.g. of bravery (p. 82)

e.g. of Ellie in love (p. 161)

Parent–child reversal

e.g of guilt (p. 95)

e.g. of emotional confusion (p. 184)

Quote—critics

Quote—Marsden

End

TWTWB shows a journey to self-discovery—both good things and bad

Making an outline for an essay

---

1 Look at the assignment again

★ This is so you don't stray off it.

---

2 What groups of ideas are here?

Hint...pick the one you'd **prefer** to write, not the one you think you **should** write.

★ If you've got ideas that point in different directions within the assignment, you might have to decide which to focus on.

★ Or you may be able to organise the ideas into a 'two-pronged' essay (see page 89).

---

3 Get some index cards

★ Normal sized index cards cut in half seem to be most user-friendly for this.

★ Write each idea on a separate card.

★ Just a word or two will do for each (enough to remind you of what the idea is).

---

4 Think about your essay's theme

Hint...let the cards point towards the theme, not the other way round.

★ Look for ideas that go together, that contradict each other, or that form a sequence.

★ From those patterns, see if a theme or argument seems to be emerging.

5 Pick out cards for a Beginning pile

Ask these questions about each card:

★ Is this a general concept about the subject of the assignment?

★ Does it give background information?

★ Is it an opinion or theory about the subject?

★ Could it be used to define or clarify the terms of the assignment?

If the answer to any of these is yes, put those cards together.

> Hint ... don't look for what a card **is**, but what it **could be**.

6 Pick out cards for a Middle pile

Ask yourself:

★ Could I use this to develop an argument or a sequence of ideas about the assignment?

★ Could I use this as evidence for one point of view, or its opposite?

★ Could I use this as an example?

If the answer to any of these is yes, put those cards together in a second pile.

7 Pick out cards for an End pile

Ask yourself:

★ Does this summarise my approach to the assignment?

★ Could I use it to draw a general conclusion?

★ Could I use it to show the overall significance of the points I've made, and how they relate to the assignment?

If the answer to any of these is yes, put those cards together.

> Hint ... you may not have any 'End' cards yet.

Keep asking: 'How can I use these ideas to address the assignment?'

8 Refine your outline

Ask yourself:

★ Can I make a 'theme' or 'summary' card?

★ Are the ideas in the Middle all pointing in the same direction (a one-pronged essay)? If so, arrange them in some logical order that relates to the assignment.

★ Are the ideas pointing in different directions, with arguments for and against, or about two different aspects of the topic (a two-pronged essay)? For more information on two-pronged essays, see page 89.

★ Are the cards in the Beginning in the best order?

Generally you want to state your broad approach first, then refer to basic information background (such as definitions or generally agreed on ideas).

★ Are the cards at the End in the best order?

(You may not have any cards for your End yet…read on.)

9 Add to the outline

Ask yourself:

Spend time rearranging the cards, and make as many 'gap fillers' as you need to.

★ Have I got big gaps that are making it hard to see an overall shape? (Solution: make temporary cards that approximately fill the gap: 'find example' or 'think of counter-argument'.)

★ Have I got plenty in one pile but nothing in another? (Solution: get whichever pile you have most cards for, into order. That will help you see where you go next, and you can make new cards as you see what's needed.)

⑩ Not working?

★ Am I stuck because I can't think of what my basic approach should be?
(Solution: start with the Middle cards and think of how these ideas can address the assignment. If one point seems stronger than the others, see if you can think of others that build on it.)

★ Am I stuck because my ideas don't connect to each other?
(Solution: find the strongest point—the one that best addresses the assignment. Then see how the other points might relate to it. They might give a different perspective, or a contradictory one, but if they connect in some way, you can use them to develop your response to the assignment.)

★ Am I stuck because I haven't got a Beginning or an End?
(Solution: make two temporary cards:

– on the first, write 'This essay will show...' and finish the sentence by summarising the information you're going to put forward, the argument you're going to make or the two points of view you're going to discuss;

– on the second, write 'This essay has shown...' and finish the sentence by recapping the information you will have given by the end of the essay, the argument you will have made, or by coming down in favour of one of the two points of view.)

These are just to complete the plan. You'll make them sound better later.

Recap

What you have now is a good idea of what your piece of writing will be about. You also have an outline that will be like a map to follow when you start writing. That's what comes next.

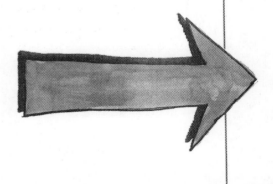

STEP FOUR
Drafting

WHEN YOU'VE GOT YOUR CATCH LAID OUT IN ORDER, YOU CAN START TO COOK IT ....

What's in STEP FOUR

About writing a first draft

One of the occupational diseases of writers is putting off the dreaded moment of actually starting to write. It's natural to want to get it right first time, but that's a big ask, so naturally you put it off some more.

However, unless you're sitting for an exam, you can do as many drafts as you need to get it right. (Some of us do quite a number: my last novel was up to draft 24 when I gave it to the publishers.) First drafts are the ones writers burn so no one can ever know how bad they were.

Only a first draft

Redrafting can seem like a chore, but you could also see it as a freedom. It means that this first draft can be as rough and 'wrong' as you like. It can also be (within reason) any length. In Step Five you'll add or cut as you need to, to make it the right length, so you don't need to worry about length at the moment.

Writing is hard if you're thinking, 'Now I am writing my piece.' That's enough to give anyone the cold horrors. It's a lot easier if you think, 'Now I am writing a first draft *of paragraph one*. Now I am writing a first draft *of paragraph two*.'

Anything you can do to make a *first* draft not feel like the *final* draft will help. Writing by hand might make it easier to write those first, foolish sentences. Promising yourself that you're not going to show this draft to a single living soul can help, too. But the very best trick I know to get going with a first draft is this: *Don't start at the beginning.*

Cleaning your room never looked so good!

Even the longest journey starts with a single step.

The GOS factor

The reason for this is the GOS factor. This is the knowledge that our piece has to have a Great Opening Sentence—one that will grip the reader from the very first moment. Probably the hardest sentence in any piece of writing is the first one (the next hardest is the GFS—the final one). Starting with the hardest sentence—the one with the biggest expectations riding on it—is enough to give you writer's block before you've written a word.

Years of my life were wasted staring at pieces of paper, trying to think of a GOS. These days, instead of agonising about that GOS, I just jot down a one-line summary to start with. I don't even think about the GOS until I've written the whole piece.

In Step Five (page 139) there's some information about how you might write a GOS—but you don't need it yet.

No matter where you start and whatever the piece is about, you need to decide *how* the piece should be written—the best **style** for its purposes. Let's take a minute to look into this idea of style.

About style

Style is a loose sort of concept that's about *how* something is written rather than *what* is written. Choosing the best style for your piece is like deciding what to wear. You probably wouldn't go to the school formal in your trackies and trainers, and it's not likely you'd go to the gym in your silk and satin. In the same way, you wouldn't use the same language for every situation. It all depends on what the piece of writing is *for*.

Writing, like clothes, is all about making choices. Let's have a
look at some of those choices:

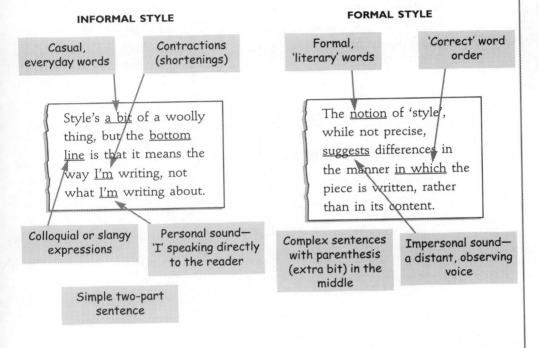

INFORMAL STYLE

Casual,
everyday words

Contractions
(shortenings)

Style's <u>a bit</u> of a woolly
thing, but the <u>bottom
line</u> is that it means the
way <u>I'm</u> writing, not
what <u>I'm</u> writing about.

Colloquial or slangy
expressions

Personal sound—
'I' speaking directly
to the reader

Simple two-part
sentence

FORMAL STYLE

Formal,
'literary' words

'Correct' word
order

The <u>notion</u> of 'style',
while not precise,
<u>suggests</u> differences in
the manner <u>in which</u> the
piece is written, rather
than in its content.

Complex sentences
with parenthesis
(extra bit) in the
middle

Impersonal sound—
a distant, observing
voice

You can see from this that style boils down to three factors:
word choice, **voice** and **sentence structure**.
    We'll look at each of those one by one.

Choice of words

English is well-supplied with synonyms—different words that mean
the same thing. They may mean the same, but you'd choose
different ones for different purposes.

The average kitchen contains *quite a few* cockroaches.
The average kitchen contains *heaps of* cockroaches.
The average kitchen contains *numerous* cockroaches.

If you were aiming to be convincing, factual and authoritative, you'd probably use 'numerous'. If you were aiming to be chatty and friendly, you might choose 'heaps'. If you were aiming for somewhere in between, you might use 'quite a few'.

Whichever one you choose is a matter of judging which one will serve your purposes best. That means thinking about the purpose of your piece and who will be reading it.

Voice

Listen to the following sentences. Who's speaking in each one?

> I hate all kinds of bugs.

This sounds personal and close up, like a person talking directly to you. It's called the first person narrator because an 'I' is speaking.

> You (reader) hate all kinds of bugs.

This narrator is telling you about yourself. This is the *second person* because the narrator is speaking *to* a second person, 'you'.

Sometimes the 'you' is not actually said, but it's there in the background, and then it sounds as if the 'you' is being given an order. For example, 'Sit down'—the 'you' is there but not actually said. This is called the imperative (meaning 'what you must do').

> He [or she] hates all kinds of bugs.

This narrator is talking about other people. It's a sort of 'onlooker'. This is the *third person* (it's talking about things happening to a third person—a 'he' or a 'she').

> One hates all kinds of bugs.

This is when you're talking about yourself, but in a disguised way—you're speaking about yourself as if you're a third person—you want to stay hidden behind a third person's mask.

This can also be used to show that you're speaking about people in general—to give the idea that it's a universal truth—for example, 'To make an omelette, one must break eggs.'

Sometimes we use 'you' as a more informal version of this 'universal' narrator, so it doesn't sound quite so pompous—for example, 'To make an omelette, you must break eggs.'

Bugs are hated.

This sentence doesn't tell us *who* hates bugs; someone does but the narrator has not told us. The narrator has rearranged the words so that bugs are the subject and focus of attention in the sentence. This is called the *passive voice*.

Computer grammar checks seem to hate the passive voice, but it has its uses. It has a certain authority. It also allows the writer to hide information from the reader—in the example above, we aren't told *who* hates bugs.

You can see from these examples that the choice you make will have a big effect on the way readers respond.

If you want your readers to be charmed, to feel relaxed, to like you, you'd probably use the personal, chatty, first-person 'I' narrator. You might use the personal voice in a letter or for a piece of imaginative writing, for example.

If you want them to be convinced by you and believe what you're saying, you'd choose a less personal narrator with more authority—the third person. You would probably use third person in an essay or a report because of its confident and objective feel.

If you want to shift the emphasis of the sentence away from the person acting, or to the action itself, you might use the passive voice. For example, in a scientific report you might say, 'A test tube was taken' or 'Four families were interviewed'.

The writer as actor, choosing a tone of voice.

Sentence structure or syntax

Syntax just means the way you put your words together to make sentences. The simplest kind of sentence has a grammatical subject, a verb and an object: 'I (subject) hate (verb) bugs (object).'

This arrangement can be varied. Sometimes you want to do something more elaborate like adding clauses and phrases, or changing the usual order of words.

> My house is full of bugs, which I hate.
>
> Bugs! I hate them.
>
> I hate bugs, although my house is full of them.
>
> Although my house is full of bugs, I hate them; however ants are different—I find them rather cute.

How to decide on the best style for your piece

Okay—so you can make a piece sound different depending on what style you choose. But how do you know what style is right for a particular piece of writing?

The answer is to go back and look again at what your piece of writing is trying to do.

You'll find more about this back on page 49, but to remind you, writing is usually trying to:

★ entertain;

★ persuade;

★ inform.

If a piece of writing is mainly setting out to **entertain**, you need to ask what style will be most entertaining for this particular piece.

Varying syntax is a way of making your writing more interesting to read.

Writing usually has several purposes—but there's usually one main purpose.

If a piece of writing is setting out to **persuade**, you need to ask what style will be most persuasive.

If you're setting out to **inform**, you need to ask what style will be best to convey information.

So, work out what your piece of writing is trying to do, then choose the best style for that purpose and write in it.

What if I can only think of one style?

Writing in different styles for different purposes assumes that you can choose between several ways of saying something. It assumes, for example, that you can think of another word for 'heaps' if you're writing an essay. But maybe you can't think of another way to say it.

One solution is to go to a thesaurus and try to find a similar word. This is okay in theory but the thesaurus won't tell you whether the word you find is going to fit with the tone of your piece. It doesn't know what kind of piece you're writing.

A different way is to use the actor all of us have inside ourselves. Try this: if you can only think of 'heaps', and you know it's too slangy for your essay, pretend you're a school principal or the prime minister and say your sentence in the tone of voice and words you'd imagine them using. If you can only think of 'numerous', but you want your piece to sound relaxed and chatty, try pretending you're on the phone to your best friend and say the sentence in the sort of words you'd probably use to him or her.

The writer as ventriloquist, using other people's voices.

The next section is about imaginative writing.
If you want to go on with essay writing, skip ahead to page 122.

First draft for imaginative writing

Styles can be combined and blended for special effect.

With imaginative writing you're trying to **entertain** your reader. You can write it in whatever style you want, from super-formal to totally slangy—whatever you think will be most 'entertaining'.

Your first decision about style might not be the right one. You'll probably know after a paragraph or two. If you need to change your mind, that's normal, because imaginative writing allows many possible styles.

The idea now is to go through the items on your outline and write each one out as a paragraph. Sometimes you can reuse some of the original writing that you did in Step One (for example, the freewriting). Mostly, you'll have to expand on it.

Show, don't tell

Think film: could you **show** this happening in a film?

Imaginative writing always works best if it's about a *particular event* rather than general or abstract thoughts. As you write out each item from the outline, make it into an incident, on a *specific day*, in a *specific place*, happening to *specific characters*.

If you can start an idea with the words 'One day...', then it's specific and therefore has a good chance of working. If not, then it might be too general, and less likely to be interesting.

This is a version of the oldest and best advice to writers: 'Show, don't tell.' *Showing* things happening, so that the reader can see the event unfolding in what feels like real time, is more interesting than you just *telling* the reader a summary of what happened. (Compare: 'I felt nervous' with 'My legs tensed up, my stomach felt fluttery and my hands were suddenly cold and clammy'.)

Write about what you know

This is good advice, too. If you try writing about characters and situations you don't know anything about, your writing will end up thin, flat and full of cliches you've borrowed from books or films. This doesn't mean you have to write about yourself. Take what you know, then give it to your characters.

Ransack your memory, stories your mother told you or something you read in the paper last week for juicy details that you can adapt for your piece.

What you know might not seem interesting to **you**—*but it will to your readers.*

Keep the flow going

Don't be stumped by the GOS—the Great Opening Sentence. If you are having trouble with this—and most of us do—give yourself a 'sound bite' that sums up the piece. Write 'This piece is basically about...' and finish the sentence in whatever words come to you. This sound bite won't be in the finished piece. It's just to remind yourself of the big picture, before you get lost in the detail.

Continue your first draft in the same way you did the freewriting in Step One (page 16). Plunge in and try not to stop. Don't keep looking back at what you've done and criticising it. You'll do that, but *later*. For now, you're just aiming to get the whole thing written out, no matter how rough it is.

Don't stop and don't look back!

Don't worry about spelling for a first draft. If you can think of a word but not how to spell it, just write it the best way you can— you'll correct it in Step Six. If you can't even think of the word, just stick in any word that will remind you of what you mean. You'll find the right word later.

Some items in your outline might take off and become several paragraphs. That's okay—let it happen. If writing is 'taking off', it's because you're interested. And if you're interested, your readers will be, too.

And don't stop and fix up bits as you write. Write the whole thing out first, otherwise you'll have a gorgeous first paragraph followed by six blank pages.

Getting stuck

We all get stuck—it's normal. The only difference between a writer and a non-writer is that writers have learned a few tricks to get unstuck.

Sometimes when you're stuck you think, I'll be okay once I get to the bit about the giraffe. Well, make it easy for yourself. Skip ahead to the bit about the giraffe. Come back later to the bit you got stuck on. You may find you don't need it, after all— you might have got stuck for the good reason that it shouldn't have been there in the first place.

There's more than one way to beat a brick wall....

How to end it

The only thing harder than a GOS is a GFS (Great Final Sentence). I had 74 goes for one of my novels. Decide that you're probably going to be writing at least six GFSs before you get one you can live with. That takes the pressure off the first one.

The end of a piece doesn't have to tie up all the threads as neatly as a parcel. It can just suggest a mood or feeling, or it can be nothing more final than a moment of equilibrium. Think of films— they often end on an image that's satisfying and suggestive, even though nothing is actually resolved. (In Step Five, page 139, there are some hints about writing a GFS.)

Don't show this first draft to anyone—not until you've got to Step Six. If you show it to people before it's properly formed, they'll all give you conflicting advice, which won't be much help at all.

First draft for imaginative writing

To remind you again, here's the assignment:

Write a piece with the title 'Steep Learning Curve'.

Deciding on a style

Since this is an imaginative writing piece, its basic job is to **entertain**. I want the reader to enjoy reading it—perhaps to identify with it. The piece can be quite personal, although it doesn't have to be about me (just a character who shares some of my experiences). And it doesn't have to be in the first person.

I'll use an informal style, with casual, everyday words. I'll use a first-person voice (though I'll reserve the right to change my mind about this as I go on). I'll keep the sentences fairly simple, but not childish.

The GOS factor

Instead of attempting a Great Opening Sentence, I'll just prop up my one-line summary in front of me as I write.

> Think I'm the only dummie
> —cheat—other girl's answers
> wrong too.

Using the outline

Turn back to page 82 to see my outline. Now I'm going to go through each card on it, developing each idea into a sentence or two.

First, the Beginning

Other kids okay, me the dummie	I always felt stupid in French classes. None of the others seemed to be having a problem, though.
Learning off by heart	I just couldn't remember the words, no matter how hard I tried.
Saying French words embarrassing	I hated having to pronounce the words in French. I knew they sounded clunky and awful.
Quote from textbook	The textbook didn't help. 'All French nouns (persons or things) are considered either masculine or feminine, the noun markers "le" and "la" (often referred to as **definite articles**) indicating the category in a distinction usually known as **gender**.'
Failing French tests	We'd had three tests so far and I'd failed them all.
Miss M trying to look French	The French teacher, let's call her Miss M, was always very smartly dressed in little suits that were just a bit too tight in the jacket. She always stood like a demonstration of 'Good Posture'. I think she was trying to look French.

French classes—like rats

We'd learned in Science about rats in cages where experimenters gave them electric shocks every time they turned on a light. After a while just the light was enough to make them squeal. There were days when I felt like that— every Wednesday and Friday morning I woke up with a headache.

Next, the Middle

`Le' and `la' problem

The `le' and `la' business had me confused. I could eventually memorise the fact that `maison' meant house. It was a bit like mansion. But what about `le' and `la'? They both meant `the', but `le' went with nouns that were called `masculine' and `la' went with words that were called `feminine'. I couldn't see anything particularly masculine or feminine about them.

Miss M unhelpful

One day, I got up courage to ask Miss M about it.

`Miss M, why is "leg" feminine and "foot" masculine?' I asked.

I was already sorry I'd asked. I felt a little stirring in the class, as if everyone was thinking, Wow, what a dummie she is. Miss M smiled—but it wasn't a friendly smile, or an understanding smile. To me it looked like a pitying smile.

`I'm afraid that's just the way they are, Louise. You just have to learn them, that's all.'

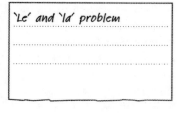

IMAGINATIVE WRITING

| Cheating | She turned away. I wasn't worth bothering with. |

She turned away. I wasn't worth bothering with. 'Now girls, a vocab test!'

My heart sank. Miss M had this thing about tests—she gave them all the time, and went around the class looking over everyone's shoulders as they did them. It was the luck of the draw, but it would be just my luck she'd pick up mine.

'The house', she said. 'The...house.'

I could remember 'mansion'. That wasn't quite right, but it was close. 'Maison'. That was it. But was it 'le' or 'la'?

'Wall. The...wall.'

Wall. Wall. I didn't have a clue.

I stared at my blank page, willing a word to come to me.

Miss M had got closer. Instead of working her way from front to back she was working her way across the room. She was only two desks away now.

How I cheated

As Caroline, the girl next to me, wrote something, I leaned back in my chair. If I leaned back just a bit further, I'd be able to see what she'd written.

What cheating felt like

I shocked myself. I was deliberately trying to cheat! I had never cheated in my life before. It had never even crossed my mind. But with Miss M getting closer, step by slow step, this was the moment I was going to start.

Caroline not letting me cheat

The trouble was, Caroline knew what I was trying to do. She leaned down, closer to the paper. Her hair swung forward and her hand curved around her work. I stared at her shoulder as I heard her pen go again. Scratch. Scratch.

> Did I want to be caught?

Miss M was quite close now. I thought she might have seen me trying to copy. I was almost glad. If they caught me cheating at French, maybe they'd let me do some other language that didn't have ridiculous masculines and feminines.

Finally, that End card

> Other girl's answers wrong too

Miss M was at the next desk now, looking hard at me. Under cover of a cough, I sort of jerked forward and accidentally-on-purpose nudged Caroline's shoulder. Just for a moment, her arm flew back and her hand uncovered the page. My eye took in at a glance what was there:

The house

The wall

Suddenly Miss M was right beside us. She picked up Caroline's paper.

'The house,' she said. 'The wall. But Caroline, I wanted the French word!'

Caroline bent her head so the hair fell forward on both sides. I suddenly understood that she felt as bad as I did about the whole French thing—worse, because it was her paper in Miss M's hand.

I wasn't such a dummie after all! Or, if I was, I wasn't the only one. It was mean of me, but I felt so relieved I almost laughed out loud. Behind us, someone sniggered, and I felt like joining in.

This is not a work of genius, and I think the End needs quite a bit more work. But at least I've got a whole story on paper now, where a while ago I didn't have any story at all.

First draft for imaginative writing

1 Decide on a style

Ask yourself:

★ Should the style be formal or casual?

★ Will I try first person or third person?

2 Write out each card in your outline

★ Start with your one-line summary of the piece. (But remember it won't appear like this in the final draft—you'll jazz it up before then.)

★ The idea is to expand each card—into a line, a paragraph or several paragraphs.

★ Within the broad shape of the item on the card, let the idea develop freely, in whatever way it wants to go (a bit like freewriting).

★ You might be able to 'lift' sections from the fragments you wrote in Step One and use them just as they are.

★ New ideas and new details will probably come to you as you write— let them.

> Hint...your outline is a guide, not a police officer.

> Hint...find a way of making a picture out of it, rather than just summarising it.

3 What if you can't think of how to expand the item?

Ask yourself:

★ Can I turn something abstract or general into something particular or specific?

★ Can I adapt something from my own life rather than inventing out of thin air?

> Hint...use people you know—including yourself— places you've been, things you've experienced.

4 What if you get stuck?

Ask yourself:

★ Am I expecting this first draft to look as polished as a final draft?
(Solution: remind yourself that the point here is just to get the whole thing written out so you can see what you've got. Then you fix it up.)

★ Am I having trouble thinking of the right word, or spelling it, or getting the sentence to come out the way I want it to?
(Solution: for the moment, just put the words down however they come to you.)

★ Is there another card further down the outline that would be easier to write out?
(Solution: leave the bit you're stuck on for the moment, and go straight to the one you feel will be easier.)

★ Am I continually reading over what I've already written?
(Solution: just plug on until you've written it all out before you go back over it.)

5 What if the story changes direction?

★ This is common—don't panic or give up.

★ Usually it means you've thought of something better than you had before. This is good!

★ Keep writing in the new direction until you can see where it's headed. Then:

★ Go back to the outline and, keeping what you can, make a new outline.

★ Resume writing, using the new outline.

What you have now is a whole piece of writing (congratulations!)—something you can now go through and fix up.

Hint...keep rearranging the cards—you'll probably be able to keep most of the original ideas.

The next section is about essay writing. If you want to go on with imaginative writing, skip ahead to Step Five (page 135).

First draft for an essay

Choosing an appropriate style

For an essay, you're trying to **persuade** or **inform** your reader. Therefore, you'll want to choose a style that makes it as persuasive or informative as possible. You want to sound as if you know what you're talking about, and that you have a considered, logical view of the assignment rather than an emotional response. Even for an essay in which you're taking sides and putting forward an argument, you'll be basing it on logic, not emotion.

This sense of your authority is best achieved by a fairly formal and impersonal style. You would probably choose:

★ reasonably formal words (not pompous ones, though);

★ no slang or colloquial words;

★ no highly emotional or prejudiced language;

★ third-person or passive voice (no 'I');

★ sentences that are grammatically correct and not overly simple (but not overly tangled, either).

In a first draft, *aim* for these features if you can, but don't get paralysed by them. It's better to go back and fix them up later (Step Six shows you how) than not to be able to write a first draft at all because you're too worried about getting it perfect.

Building paragraphs

The idea now is to go through the items on your outline and write out each one as a new paragraph. (Some items may turn into more than one paragraph.)

The voice of quiet authority.

In general, each paragraph in an essay should have these three elements:

★ a **topic sentence** that acts like a headline, saying what the paragraph will be about;

★ a **development** of this idea—where you insert the details about it;

★ **supporting material** in the form of examples, evidence or quotes.

A paragraph is like a tiny story in itself.

The topic sentence might also show where the paragraph fits with the one before it. You might show this with signal words like 'First…' 'Second…' 'On the other hand…' that guide the reader around your work. (See Step Five for more of these.)

Somewhere in each paragraph of the first draft, it's a good idea to use the key word from the assignment, so that each idea is firmly shown to be relevant. This will seem very heavy-handed, but when you revise in Step Five, you can decide whether to delete a few uses of the key word to make your argument more subtle.

Using your outline

As you write, you might see ways to improve or add to your outline. Change it, but make sure it's still addressing the assignment and moving in a logical way from point to point. Don't let yourself be drawn down paths that aren't relevant to the assignment.

Keeping the flow going

Postpone that intimidating GOS—Great Opening Sentence. Instead, use the one-line summary of your basic idea that you put at the head of your outline in Step Three. This sentence won't appear in

Sidestep the hardest part.

the final essay—it's probably pretty dull. You'll think of a more interesting way to start the essay in Step Five.

Plunge in and try not to stop until you've roughed-out the whole piece.

If you can't think of the right word, put any word you can think of that is close to what you want to convey. If you're desperate, you can always leave a blank. If you've forgotten a date or a name, leave a blank and come back to it later. Get spelling and grammar right if you can—but don't let those things stop you. Don't go back and fix things. Rough the whole thing out now and fix the details later.

Getting stuck

The Beginning of an essay is often a hard place to start. It's where the central issue of the essay is presented—whether it's a body of information about a subject, or a particular argument. Sometimes it's hard to write this before you've written the whole piece. If you're finding this is the case, write the Middle first. Come back later when you can see what you've done and tackle the Beginning. (In Step Five, page 139, there's some information about getting that GOS right, but you don't need it now.)

How to end it

Ending an essay can be almost as hard as starting it. The pressure is on for that Great Final Sentence to be—well—great. Take the pressure off for now. Just draw together the points you've made in the best final paragraph you can. You'll probably need more than one try before you get it exactly right—don't spend too much time on it now. (Step Five is the time for that.)

Don't give this to a reader yet. It's rough, and they might not be able to see past the roughness to the shape underneath. Revise it first (Step Five), otherwise you might be unnecessarily discouraged.

A blank space can be a writer's best friend!

'How can I know what I think, until I've heard myself say it?'

Showing a reader a first draft can be hard on everyone.

First draft for an essay

Here's my topic again:

> 'Every story is a journey towards self-discovery.' Using as an example a novel you've read this year, show why you agree or disagree with this statement.

Deciding on a style

I'll aim for a middle-of-the-road essay style: fairly formal and written in the third person.

The GOS factor

Rather than agonise about a GOS, I'll prop my one-line summary of the essay up in front of me so I can keep checking I'm still on course as I write:

> Summary: Agree with statement: TWTWB a journey towards self-discovery—both good things and bad

Using the outline

Turn back to page 97 to see the outline. Now I'm going to go through each card on it, developing each idea into a sentence, a paragraph, or several paragraphs. To make sure I stay on track, I'll frequently use key words from the assignment.

First, the Beginning

Summary: Agree with statement: TWTWB a journey towards self-discovery—both good things and bad	This essay will show that <u>Tomorrow, When the War Began</u> shows a journey to self-discovery—discovery of good qualities and bad.
TWTWB a good example	<u>Tomorrow, When the War Began</u> is a good example of a book in which 'a journey of self-discovery' takes place. In the course of the book, the main character, Ellie, goes through several different kinds of self-discovery as she responds to the frightening and violent things that are happening around her.
Dictionary definition	The <u>Macquarie Dictionary</u> defines 'discovery' as 'discover: To get knowledge of, learn of, or find out; gain sight or knowledge of something previously unseen or unknown.'
S-d implies you didn't know before	Self-discovery implies learning something previously unknown about yourself.
S-d can be about good things	Self-discovery can mean learning good things about yourself.

S-d can be about bad things

You can also discover things about yourself that are not so good.

S-d needs a crisis

It's because of the extreme and dangerous events in the book that Ellie comes to learn new things about herself.

Now the cards for the Middle

e.g. of bravery (p. 82)

In the course of the book, Ellie makes discoveries about good qualities in herself. Her first discovery about herself comes about soon after the teenagers come back from a camping trip and find their families have been locked up in the showground. They need to get close to the showground, and have to come out of the shadows to get close enough to see what's going on. Ellie is not sure she has the guts for this. She says: 'To come out of the darkness now would be to show courage of a type that I'd never had to show before. I had to search my own mind and body to find if there was a new part of me somewhere' (p. 81). Finally she brings herself to do so and says: 'I felt then, and still feel now, that I was transformed by those four steps...I started becoming someone else, a more complicated and capable person...' (p. 82).

e.g. of love—Ellie in love
(p. 16)

Over the course of the book, Ellie develops an interest in two of the boys in the group and is surprised by her feelings—another example of positive self-discovery. What she's feeling for Homer and Lee feels like a new aspect of herself—especially what she feels for Lee: 'It was all happening too unexpectedly...Lee was so intense he scared me, but at the same time I felt something strong when he was around—I just didn't know what it was.'

Parent—child reversal

The parent—child roles are reversed after the invasion, and the young people are the ones left to make decisions. This is another kind of positive self-discovery. This contrasts with before the invasion— the book opens with all the young people trying to persuade their parents to let them go on the camping trip. But as the reality sinks in, Ellie wonders how her parents reacted to the invasion. She says, 'I hoped they'd been sensible' (p. 78)— more often what a parent thinks about a child.

e.g. of guilt (p. 95)

During the book Ellie discovers some negative qualities in herself. One of the first moments of violence in the book is when Ellie blows up three soldiers with a lawnmower. Telling the others about it, they listen as she says: 'I began to have trouble—It was hard for me to believe that I had probably just killed three people. It was too big a thing for me to get my mind around. I was so filled with horror. I felt guilty and ashamed about what had happened' (p. 95). In fact, she thought she might have changed into 'a raging monster' (p. 161).

e.g. of emotional confusion
(p. 184)

She doesn't like finding both Lee and Homer attractive: 'I didn't have any plans to become the local slut...' (p. 161) and tries to deny her feelings. She wants things to be simple and clearcut, and is disturbed by feeling attracted to both at once. She realises that part of the reason she's disturbed is that she likes to be in control: 'I guess I like to be in control' (p. 183), but she's forced to recognise that when it comes to attraction to someone else, she can't be in control.

From thinking she knew herself quite well, she has to admit: 'I'm all confused' (p. 184).

Quote—critics

The critics Nimon and Foster point out that the characters have 'actually gained something by their involvement in the war—the characters realise how they have matured and developed' (p. 177). The journey to self-discovery that Ellie takes would not happen unless the traumatic events took place.

Quote—Marsden

On his website, John Marsden says that one of the factors in his mind as he wrote the book was 'watching an Anzac Day Parade and wondering how today's teenagers would react if they were placed in the same position as their grandparents and great-grandparents...I was fairly sure that given a challenge the teenagers of the nineties would show as much courage and maturity as their predecessors.'

In _Tomorrow, When the War Began_, he shows a group of young people coming through adversity and violence to a greater awareness of themselves and what they are capable of.

Now for the End

> TWTWB shows a journey to
> self-discovery

The narrator of <u>Tomorrow, When the War Began</u>, Ellie, goes through a journey of self-discovery over the pages of the book, learning about many aspects of her personality which she was not aware of previously. Many of these are aspects she can be proud of, but one of the disturbing qualities of the book is that Ellie discovers that there are also dark places in her which she has to come to terms with. On balance, she ends up a better person because of her self-discoveries.

This is not wonderful, but at least I've got a complete essay, where an hour ago I had no essay at all. All the things that are wrong with it can be fixed, and that's what I'll do in Steps Five and Six.

First draft for an essay

1 Remind yourself of the 'essay style'

Aim to use:

★ formal, non-slangy words;

★ third person or, for certain kinds of essays, passive voice;

★ grammatically correct sentences that aren't too simplistic.

2 Write out each card on your outline

★ Start with your one-line summary of the piece. (But remember it won't appear like this in the final draft—this is just to give you a run-up. When you've written the essay out, you can come back and think of a better way to start it.)

★ The idea is to expand each card into a paragraph (or several paragraphs).

★ In general, each card should be a new paragraph (this might not be true of the Beginning and End sections).

> Hint...don't get bogged down thinking of exactly the right words— fix them later.

3 Structure each paragraph

Use:

★ a **topic sentence** which says what the paragraph will be about;

★ a **development** which gives more details, in a few sentences;

★ **evidence** which gives examples or other supporting material.

4 **Link each paragraph to the assignment**

Ask yourself:

★ How does this help to address the assignment I've been given?

★ How can I *show* that it addresses the assignment?

★ How can I connect this paragraph to the one before?

> Hint...spell out the relevance clearly in this draft. If it's too heavy-handed you can lighten it later.

5 **What if you can't think of how to expand on a card?**

Ask yourself:

★ Should this idea be in the essay after all?

★ Do I need to find out some more information?
  If so, more research might give you what you need.

★ Does this point need some support or proof?
  If so, go and look for some. If you can't find anything, consider whether you should still include that point.

> Hint...maybe it's not really relevant or not important enough to include.

6 **What if you get stuck?**

Ask yourself:

★ Am I feeling anxious because this doesn't sound like an essay?
  (Solution: it's not an *essay* yet. It's only a *first draft*. Give it time.)

★ Am I having trouble thinking of the right word or right spelling?
  (Solution: for the moment, just find the best approximation you can. Fix it up later.)

★ Am I stuck because I've forgotten a date or name or technical term?
  (Solution: leave a blank and look it up when you've finished writing this draft.)

★ Am I stuck because my sentence has become long and tangled up in itself?
  (Solution: cut the sentence up into several short, simpler ones.)

★ Do I keep going back and re-reading what I've done?
(Solution: just press ahead and get it all down before you go back.)

★ Is there another card further down the outline that would be easier to write about?
(Solution: leapfrog down to that card. Start the writing for it on a new page, though, and don't forget to go back later and fill in the gap.)

★ Do I keep losing sight of how each idea is relevant?
(Solution: use key words from the assignment in each topic sentence.)

> Hint...
> remember, this draft is for **your eyes** only. Just press on!

7 What if the essay changes direction?

★ This is common, so don't panic—although a well-planned outline will help prevent it.

★ Once you can see the new direction, stop writing and go back to the assignment. Would this new direction be a better way to approach the assignment after all?

★ If you think so, go back to the index cards. Add new ones for the new ideas, cut out any that no longer fit, and rearrange the rest if you need to.

★ Resume writing using the new outline and remind yourself to spend more time outlining the next time you write an essay.

> Hint...when you're doing this you may see that in fact the new direction isn't all that different from the first one.

Recap

What you have now is a whole essay (congratulations!)—something you can go through and fix up where necessary. That's what the last two steps are about.

STEP FIVE

Revising

trim a bit off here, add a pinch of
this and that and REARRANGE UNTIL
it looks good ...

About revising

You've now got a piece of writing instead of a blank page and a sinking feeling in your stomach. You know that what you're supposed to do now is **revise** it. But what does revising really mean?

Revising literally means 're-seeing'. It is about fixing the bigger, structural problems and, if necessary, 're-seeing' the whole shape of the piece. What this boils down to is finding places where you need to **cut** something out, places where you should **add** something, and places where you need to **move** or rearrange something.

Revising doesn't mean fixing surface problems such as grammar and spelling. That's what's called 'editing', and we'll get to that in Step Six.

Two-step revising

There are two quite different things you have to do when revising. It's tempting to try to do them both at the same time, but it's quicker in the long run to do them one by one.

The first thing is to **find** the problems. The second thing is to **fix** them.

Finding problems

Coming to your own work fresh is one of the hardest things about writing. Somehow, you have to put aside everything you know about the background of the piece—what you intended, the real situation it might be based on—and react to what *you've actually got on the paper*.

If you want to find problems before your readers do, you have to try to read it the way they will. That means reading it *straight through* without stopping, to get a feeling for the piece as a whole. Read it aloud if you can—it will sound quite different and you'll hear where things should be changed.

Revising = re-seeing. Editing = polishing the surface.

Read like a cold-hearted stranger.

Don't waste this read-through by stopping to fix things, but read with a pen in your hand. When you come to something that doesn't quite feel right, put a squiggle in the margin beside it, then keep reading.

Trust your gut feeling. If *you* feel that there's something wrong—even if you don't know what it is—your readers will too.

Time helps you come to a piece freshly. Even fifteen minutes—while you take the dog for a walk—helps you get some distance on what you've written.

If you're working on a computer, I strongly recommend that you print it out (double-spaced) before you start revising. Things always look better on the screen—more like a finished product. But right now you don't want them to look any better than they really are—you want to *find* problems, not *hide* them.

The first time you read the piece through, think only about these questions:

★ Have I *repeated myself* here or waffled on?

★ Is there *something missing* here?

★ Are parts of this in the *wrong order*?

Fixing problems

After you've read the piece through, go back to each of the squiggles you made, and work out just why it didn't sound right.

★ If you repeated something, you need to **cut**.

★ If you're missing something, you'll need to **add**.

★ If parts are in the wrong order, you'll need to **move** things around.

If the problem is something else—spelling or grammar, for example—leave it for the moment. You'll fix those in Step Six.

A copy makes it easier to be ruthless.

Revising = big-picture stuff:
• cutting
• adding
• moving.

The Great Opening Sentence (GOS)

Now it is time to replace your 'summary' sentence with a GOS. A GOS should get your reader interested, but not give too much away. A good GOS will often make the reader ask 'Why?'—then they'll read on, to find the answer to that question.

There are two ways to come up with a GOS. One way is to **find** it. It may be embedded somewhere in your piece, already written—read through the piece, auditioning each sentence (or part of it) for a starring role as a GOS. Or you may find it somewhere else—a sentence in another piece of writing may suggest a GOS, or the sentence may be useable as a direct quote.

The other way to produce a GOS is to **write** it. Approach this in the same way as you got ideas in Step One—let your mind think sideways and don't reject any suggestions. Write down all the openers you can dream up, no matter how hopeless they seem. When you've got a page covered with attempts, circle the ones that seem most promising—or just a good phrase or word—and build on these. Assume that you'll write many GOS attempts before you come up with a good one.

The Great Final Sentence (GFS)

It's time to get that right, too. A GFS should leave the reader feeling that all the different threads of the piece have been drawn together in a satisfying way. A piece might end with a powerful final statement, or in a quiet way. In either case, the reader should feel sure this is the end—not just that there's a page missing.

As with the GOS, you may find your GFS hiding somewhere in what you've already written, or you may need to write one from scratch. Go about it in the same way as you did for the GOS.

The next section is about imaginative writing.
If you want to go on with essay writing, skip ahead to page 153.

Revising imaginative writing

A piece of imaginative writing is aiming to **entertain**, or keep the reader interested. As you read through your draft, you'll be looking for changes that will make the piece *more* entertaining: changes that would make the reader laugh more, cry more or want more desperately to know what happened next.

Once you've identified the places that don't feel quite right, you have to decide whether to **cut**, **add** or **move**.

Cutting

'Cut to the chase.'

Here are some things that might need to be cut:

★ unnecessary background information (for example, starting the story too far back, so it begins too slowly);

★ over-long dialogue (less is more with dialogue);

★ dull 'nuts and bolts'—getting the characters from A to B;

★ descriptions of characters that only tell your readers what colour their eyes are, not *who* they are;

★ things that have already been said;

★ things that readers have already worked out for themselves;

★ anti-climactic endings that keep going after the audience has left the show.

Adding

Here are some things that might need to be added:

★ something that *you* know but haven't told the reader (the age or sex of the narrator, for example);

★ a picture that *you* have in *your* mind's eye but have only summarised for the reader (where you've *told* instead of *shown*). For example, 'It was a shabby house'—a summary—could become 'Tiles were missing from the roof and the verandah sagged at one end...'—a picture;

★ extensions to parts that were just getting interesting;

★ material that balances the story better (for example, if it takes a long time to set the scene then the main action is rushed);

★ the kind of detail that makes a story come to life: the personality of characters, the atmosphere of a setting, significant details;

★ dialogue which can enliven a dull story and speed up a slow one;

★ a punchier opening and/or ending—adding the GOS and the GFS.

Moving

Here are some things that might need to be moved around:

★ parts of the story that jump backwards and forwards in time in a confusing way;

★ parts of the story that jump between characters in a confusing way;

★ dull background information that interrupts a dramatic moment;

★ essential background information that's given too late;

★ a static opening (for example, a long description) that could be moved into the body of the story;

★ parts where the climax or a secret is given away too soon, which would be better placed later.

It's tempting to talk yourself out of the need for major surgery. On a second reading, you might think 'Oh, that looks okay after all'. Don't be fooled. A *first* reading is all this piece will get from most readers.

Fill in the blanks.

The right words in the wrong place.

If it felt like a problem on the first read-through, then it's a problem.

No writer likes to have to cut anything. My solution is to put cuts into a folder called 'Good bits to use later' or something like that. Then you can go ahead and be as ruthless as you need to be without feeling you've wasted something.

Other ways to revise

Sometimes, adding, cutting or moving doesn't quite do the job. For imaginative writing, it sometimes helps to rewrite the piece, or a part of it, without looking at your first draft. Skim through it quickly, but then put it away and rewrite it. If it starts to go in a somewhat different direction, let it—see where the new version wants to go.

As you continue your revisions you might decide that you were right in an earlier version, and you need to go back to that. In fact, you might end up doing a number of drafts, and your final piece might be a combination of all of them. For this reason, it's a good idea to keep a copy of each rewrite you do. If you're working on paper, this just means keeping all copies. If you're working on a computer, make a copy before you start changing it.

Revising 'too much'

Writing students often ask me about the danger of 'overworking' a piece—revising it so much it loses its spontaneity and freshness. Without being rude, I try to tell them that this is just another avoidance technique. (We writers know them all!)

Writing nearly always gets better with every draft. Rather than being a chore, revising can be the best bit of writing. You're not producing something out of thin air any more. You can enjoy tinkering around with it, trying it this way, trying it that way...and with every change you make, the piece will get better.

If you were right the first time...

You're not being fair to your writing if you haven't done three drafts (at least!).

Revising imaginative writing

Here's my first draft from Step Four with squiggles added when I did my first read-through. The instructions **add**, **cut** and **move** were added on a second reading.

First draft

> Move

> Add GOS

I always felt stupid in French classes. None of the others seemed to be having a problem, though.

> Add connectors

I just couldn't remember the words, no matter how hard I tried.

I hated having to pronounce the words in French. I knew they sounded clunky and awful.

> Move

The textbook didn't help. `All French nouns (persons or things) are considered either masculine or feminine, the noun markers "le" and "la" (often referred to as definite articles) indicating the category in a distinction usually known as gender.'

> Move

We'd had three tests so far and I'd failed them all.

The French teacher, let's call her Miss M, was always very smartly dressed in little suits that were just a bit too tight in the jacket.

> Cut

She always stood like a demonstration of `Good Posture'. I think she was trying to look French.

> Move

We'd learned in Science about rats in cages where experimenters gave them electric shocks every time they turned on a light. After a while just the light was enough to make them squeal. There were days when I felt like that—every Wednesday and Friday morning I woke up with a headache.

> Add connector

The `le' and `la' business had me confused. I could eventually memorise the fact that `maison' meant house. It was a bit like mansion. But what about `le' and `la'? They both meant `the', but `le' went with nouns that were called `masculine' and `la' went with words that were called `feminine'. I couldn't see anything particularly masculine or feminine about them.

> Add (name)

> Move

One day, I got up courage to ask <u>Miss M</u> about it.

IMAGINATIVE WRITING

Add name →

'Miss M, why is 'leg' feminine and 'foot' masculine?' I asked.

I was already sorry I'd asked. I felt a little stirring in the class, as if everyone was thinking, Wow, what a dummie she is. Miss M smiled—but it wasn't a friendly smile, or an understanding smile. To me it looked like a pitying smile.

'I'm afraid that's just the way they are, Louise. You just have to learn them, that's all.'   ← Cut

She turned away. I wasn't worth bothering with.

'Now girls, a vocab test!'

Add name →

My heart sank. Miss M had this thing about tests—she gave them all the time, and went around the class looking over everyone's shoulders as they did them. It was the luck of the draw, but it   ← Cut
would be just my luck she'd pick up mine.

'The house', she said. 'The...house.'

I could remember 'mansion'. That wasn't quite right, but it was close. Maison. That was it. But was it 'le' or 'la'?

'Wall. The...wall.'

Wall. Wall. I didn't have a clue.

I stared at my blank page, willing a word to come to me.

Add name →

Miss M had got closer. Instead of working her way from front to back she was working her way across the room. She was only two desks away now.

As Caroline, the girl next to me, wrote something, I leaned back   ← Add smoothers
in my chair. If I leaned back just a bit further, I'd be able to see what she'd written.

Add name →

I shocked myself. I was deliberately trying to cheat! I had never cheated in my life before. It had never even crossed my mind. But   ← Add smoothers
with Miss M getting closer, step by slow step, this was the moment I was going to start.

The trouble was, Caroline knew what I was trying to do. She

Add →

leaned down, closer to the paper. Her hair swung forward and her hand curved around her work. I stared at her shoulder as I heard her   ← Move
pen go again. Scratch. Scratch.

IMAGINATIVE WRITING

Add name

Add

Add smoothers

Cut

Move

Add name

Add smoothers

Cut

Cut/move

Add ending

Add GFS

Miss M was quite close now. I thought she might have seen me trying to copy. I was almost glad. If they caught me cheating at French, maybe they'd let me do some other language that didn't have ridiculous masculines and feminines.

Miss M was at the next desk now, looking hard at me. Under cover of a cough, I sort of jerked forward and accidentally-on-purpose nudged Caroline's shoulder. Just for a moment, her arm flew back and her hand uncovered the page. My eye took in at a glance what was there:

The house

The wall

Suddenly Miss M was right beside us. She picked up Caroline's paper.

'The house,' she said. 'The wall. But Caroline, I wanted the French word!'

Caroline bent her head so the hair fell forward on both sides. I suddenly understood that she felt as bad as I did about the whole French thing—worse, because it was her paper in Miss M's hand.

I wasn't such a dummie after all! Or, if I was, I wasn't the only one. It was mean of me, but I felt so relieved I almost laughed out loud. Behind us, someone sniggered, and I felt like joining in.

Second draft

Changes are shown in bold type.

> **It was getting so I was frightened of French classes. None of the** other kids seemed to be having a problem, but I always felt stupid. We'd had three tests so far and I'd failed them all.
>
> **For a start**, I just couldn't remember the words, no matter how hard I tried. **Plus**, I hated having to pronounce the words in French. I knew they sounded clunky and awful.
>
> **The French teacher was always very smartly dressed** in little suits that were just a bit too tight in the jacket. **I think she was trying to look French.**
>
> **We'd learned in Science about rats in cages, where experimenters gave them electric shocks every time they turned on a light. After a while just the light was enough to make them squeal. There were days when I felt like that—every Wednesday and Friday morning I woke up with a headache.**
>
> **The textbook didn't help.** 'All French nouns (persons or things) are considered either masculine or feminine, the noun markers 'le' and 'la' (often referred to as **definite articles**) indicating the category in a distinction usually known as **gender.**'
>
> **This** 'le' and 'la' business had me confused. I could eventually memorise the fact that 'maison' meant house. It was a bit like 'mansion'. But what about 'le' and 'la'? They both meant 'the', but 'le' went with nouns that were called 'masculine' and 'la' went with words that were called 'feminine'.
>
> One day, I got up courage to ask Miss **Marshall** about it.
>
> 'Miss **Marshall**, why is 'leg' feminine and 'foot' masculine?' I asked.
>
> I felt a little stirring in the class, as if everyone was thinking, Wow! What a dummie she is. I was already sorry I'd asked. Miss **Marshall** smiled—but it wasn't a friendly smile, or an understanding smile. To me it looked like a pitying smile.

'I'm afraid that's just the way they are, Louise.' **She turned away**. I wasn't worth bothering with. 'Now girls, a vocab test!'

My heart sank. Miss **Marshall** had this thing about tests—she gave them all the time, and went around the class **looking over everyone's shoulders as they did them.**

'The house', she said. 'The...house.'

I could remember 'mansion'. That wasn't quite right, but it was close. 'Maison'. That was it. But was it 'le' or 'la'?

'Wall. The...wall.'

Wall. Wall. I didn't have a clue.

I stared at my blank page, willing a word to come to me.

Miss **Marshall** had got closer. Instead of working her way from front to back she was working her way across the room. She was only two desks away now.

I could hear Caroline, the girl next to me, writing. I stared at her shoulder as I heard her pen go again. Scratch. Scratch. I realised that, if I leaned back just a bit further, I'd be able to see what she'd written.

I shocked myself. I was deliberately trying to cheat! **In my whole life, it had never even crossed my mind to cheat.** It had never even crossed my mind. But with Miss Marshall getting closer, step by slow step, this was the moment I was going to start.

The trouble was that Caroline knew what I was trying to do. She leaned down, closer to the paper. Her hair swung forward and her hand curved around her work.

Miss **Marshall** was quite close now, **looking hard at me.** I thought she might have seen me trying to copy **and** I was almost glad. If they caught me cheating at French, maybe they'd let me do some other language that didn't have ridiculous masculines and feminines.

Under cover of a cough, I jerked forward and accidentally-on-purpose nudged Caroline's shoulder. Just for a moment, her arm flew back and her hand uncovered the page. My eye took in at a glance what was there:

The house

The wall

Suddenly Miss **Marshall** was right beside **us, picking up** Caroline's paper.

'The house,' she said. 'The wall. But Caroline, **this is in English!**

Caroline bent her head so the hair fell forward on both sides. I suddenly understood that she felt as bad as I did about the whole French thing—worse, because it was her paper in Miss **Marshall's** hand.

I wasn't such a dummie after all! Or, if I was, I wasn't the only one. **Behind us, someone sniggered, and I was so relieved** I felt like joining in.

I didn't exactly plan it, but I found my hand had gone up in the air.

'Miss Marshall, I don't think I understand any of this...The words. How you remember them. And the 'le' and 'la' thing.'

The silence that followed seemed like the longest silence that had ever happened in the whole history of the planet.

'You want me to explain it all again?'

I felt relieved. There was nothing to dread anymore, because the worst was actually happening.

She looked around at the rest of the class, all sitting as still as a photograph, staring at us.

'Hands up anyone else who needs to have it explained again.'

There was another long silence. In different parts of the room, small parts of bodies shifted: a hand moved along a desk here, a shoulder shifted there, someone leaned back over there. A hand rose towards head-level, but it could have been to scratch an ear. Another elbow came up, but perhaps just to free a tight sleeve. Like a time-lapse movie of grass sprouting, hands slowly rose all over the room, until every single girl had her hand in the air.

That was when Miss Marshall started to laugh. We'd never seen her laugh before.

> 'Okay, girls. The first thing you need to know about French is that it's a pig of a language to learn.'
> She perched on the side of the desk.
> 'That's where we'll start.'

This still isn't brilliant—it's a little bit too much the 'happy ending'—but at least it's an ending. The whole piece would improve with a few more rewrites, but at least this second draft is a bit better than the first.

Revising imaginative writing

1 Make a copy of the first draft

★ This is so you can scribble on it to your heart's content.

★ Space it generously so you can read it easily.

2 Read like a stranger

★ Don't stop and fix things.

★ If something sounds wrong, mark it with a squiggle in the margin.

★ Don't stop to work out *why* it sounds wrong.

3 Consider making cuts

On a second reading, ask yourself:

Hint...you can change your mind later, and put them back in!

★ Should I 'cut to the chase' and lose some of the introduction?

★ Should I 'ring down the curtain' and cut an anti-climactic ending?

★ Should I cut, or tighten, the dialogue?

★ Should I cut some of the description?

★ Have I already said this?

★ Would the reader have already worked this out?

★ Can I cut any dull 'nuts and bolts' details?

4 **Consider adding something**

Ask yourself:

★ Have I assumed that the readers know something I haven't actually told them?

★ Have I summarised rather than drawn a picture (**told** rather than **shown**)?

★ Is there an interesting bit that is too brief?

★ Is the piece lopsided (for example, with too much description/not enough action)?

★ Should I develop characters or atmosphere with more vivid details?

★ Do I need a GOS or a GFS?

> Hint...if you add too much now, you can always cut it later.

5 **Consider moving parts around**

Ask yourself:

★ Could I rearrange things to smooth out confusing jumps in time?

★ Could I rearrange parts to prevent confusing movements between characters?

★ Have I interrupted a strong dramatic moment with some static background information?

★ Have I left it too late to tell the readers something they need to know?

★ Have I given away the climax or the secret too early so there are no surprises for the reader?

> Hint... sometimes a diagram of the piece helps.

6 What if you can see a problem but not how to fix it?

Ask yourself:

★ Is it that I can't make myself cut something out?
(Solution: tell yourself a little white lie—use your 'Good bits I'll use later' folder.)

★ Is it that I can't think of anything to add?
(Solutions:

- Go back to the idea-starters in Step One.

- Tune into the world around you: the man on the bus next to you might have just the right kind of face for your character; he might be having just the conversation you need for your dialogue.

- Do more research to find interesting details.)

★ Am I afraid I'll get in a muddle when I start moving things around?
(Solution: cut the writing up physically and put it together in a new order with sticky-tape. Primitive, but it works—and why your other copy comes in handy.)

★ Is it that my GOS isn't working?
(Solution: read through the piece, trying out each sentence in your mind as the opening sentence. The GOS may be embedded in the body of the piece. If this doesn't work, you'll have to write one. A good GOS is often a very short sentence with a vivid image or idea. Be prepared to have quite a few attempts, and to think laterally.)

> Hint...this is why you made a copy, back at the beginning.

The next section is about essay writing. If you want to go on with imaginative writing, skip ahead to Step Six (page 165).

Revising an essay

An essay will generally be aiming to give the readers **information**, or **persuade** them of something. As you read through your draft, you'll be looking for changes that will help readers understand the information better or be more convinced by your argument. Once you've found the places that need fixing, you have to decide whether to **cut**, **add** or **move**.

Cutting

Here are some things that might need cutting:

- ★ padding—too little information or argument taking up too much space;
- ★ waffle—pompous or over-elaborate sentences with no real purpose;
- ★ repeated ideas or information;
- ★ irrelevant material (even if it's brilliant or took you hours to write, it has to address the assignment);
- ★ words, sentences or even whole ideas if the essay is longer than required.

Padding—great in an armchair, not in an essay.

Adding

Here are some things that might need be added:

- ★ information that you've assumed but not actually stated (don't rely on the reader to fill the gaps);
- ★ a step in your argument that you've left out;
- ★ details or explanations that show how your ideas relate to the assignment;

The missing
links.

★ connectors or pointers that smooth the flow between your
ideas;

★ the introduction and conclusion: this is the moment to
compose a GOS and a GFS.

Moving

Here are some things that might need to be moved around:

Right idea,
wrong place.

★ information that's not in the most logical order (for example,
from most important to least important, most distant in time
to most recent, or any order that works and is consistent);

★ information that's important but is given to the reader at the
wrong time (for example, background information that
should go before the main argument);

★ steps in an argument that are not, in the most logical order
(an argument has to build up step by step, with the evidence
for each step, and then a final, convincing statement);

★ something that is good
in itself but interrupts
the flow;

★ the arrangement in a two-
pronged essay (see page
89); you may decide now
that you made the wrong
choice and need to
rearrange some of
the parts.

GReat Idea — but is it
packaged the Right way?

Other ways to revise

Sometimes cutting, adding or moving doesn't quite do the trick. If that's the case, put the draft away and simply tell someone (real or imaginary) what it's about. Then tell them the contents of each paragraph, one by one. (You might start with words like 'What I'm saying here is…') Then write down what you've just heard yourself say. Those words will give you a clear, simply-worded version of your essay which you can then embellish with details from your written draft.

Revising 'too much'

It's easy to talk yourself out of the need to make changes. On a second reading some of the problems appear to melt away. You've got to remember, though, that most pieces don't get a second reading.

Nevertheless, as you continue your revisions, you might decide you were right in an earlier version and you need to go back to that. It's a good idea not to delete or throw away any parts of your earlier drafts—keep them somewhere, in case. (For computer work, make a copy before you start changing it.)

Don't worry about 'overworking' a piece until you've revised it at least three times. An overworked essay is a rare and seldom-sighted creature.

Strange though it seems, revising can actually be the best part of writing. You've done the hard work—you've actually created an essay out of thin air. You don't have to do that again. Now you can enjoy tinkering with it, adding here, cutting there—getting the whole thing as good as you can make it.

Back to basics.

If something felt like a problem on the first reading, it *is* a problem.

Revising an essay

Here's the first draft of my essay as it was at the end of Step Four, with the squiggles added when I did my very first read-through. The instructions—**add**, **cut** and **move**—were added on a second reading.

First draft

Add better GOS	This essay will show that <u>Tomorrow, When the War Began</u> shows a journey to self-discovery—discovery of good qualities and bad. ◄ **Add smoother**
Add background info	<u>Tomorrow, When the War Began</u> is a good example of a book in which 'a journey of self-discovery' takes place. In the course of the book, the main character, Ellie, goes through several different kinds of self-discovery as she responds to the frightening and violent things that are happening around her.
Add smoothers	The <u>Macquarie Dictionary</u> defines 'discovery' as 'discover: To get knowledge of, learn of, or find out; gain sight or knowledge of something previously unseen or unknown.'
	Self-discovery implies learning something previously unknown about yourself.
	Self-discovery can mean learning good things about yourself. You can also discover things about yourself that are not so good.
Cut	It's because of the extreme and dangerous events in the book that Ellie comes to learn new things about herself.
Add connector	In the course of the book, Ellie makes discoveries about good qualities in herself. Her first discovery about herself comes about soon after the teenagers come back from a camping trip and find their families have been locked up in the showground. They need to get close to the showground, and have to come out of the shadows **Cut** to get close enough to see what's going on. Ellie is not sure she has the guts for this. She says: 'To come out of the darkness now would be to show courage of a type that I'd never had to show before.

I had to search my own mind and body to find if there was a new part of me somewhere' (p. 81). Finally she brings herself to do so and says: 'I felt then, and still feel now, that I was transformed by those four steps...I started becoming someone else, a more complicated and capable person...' (p. 82).

[Add connector] → Over the course of the book, Ellie develops an interest in two of the boys in the group and is surprised by her feelings—another example of positive self-discovery: 'It was all happening too unexpectedly...Lee was so intense he scared me, but at the same time I felt something strong when he was around—I just didn't know what it was' (p. 183). **[Cut]** What she's feeling for Homer and Lee feels like a new aspect of herself—especially what she feels for Lee. **[Cut]**

[Add connector] → The parent-child roles are reversed after the invasion, and the young people are the ones left to make decisions. This is another kind of positive self-discovery. This contrasts with before the invasion—the book opens with all the young people trying to persuade their parents to let them go on the camping trip. But as the reality sinks in, Ellie wonders how her parents reacted to the invasion. She says, 'I hoped they'd been sensible' (p. 78)—more often what a parent thinks about a child.

One of the first moments of violence in the book is when Ellie **[Add 'You are here']** blows up three soldiers with a lawnmower. Telling the others about it, they listen as she says: 'I began to have trouble—It was hard for me to believe that I had probably just killed three people. It was too big a thing for me to get my mind around...I was so filled with horror...I felt guilty and ashamed about what had happened' (p. 95). In fact she thought she might have changed into 'a raging monster' (p. 161).

She doesn't like finding both Lee and Homer attractive, 'I didn't **[Add connector]** have any plans to become the local slut...' (p. 161) and tries to deny her feelings. She wants things to be simple and clearcut, and is disturbed by feeling attracted to both at once. She realises that **[Cut]** part of the reason she's disturbed is that she likes to be in control:

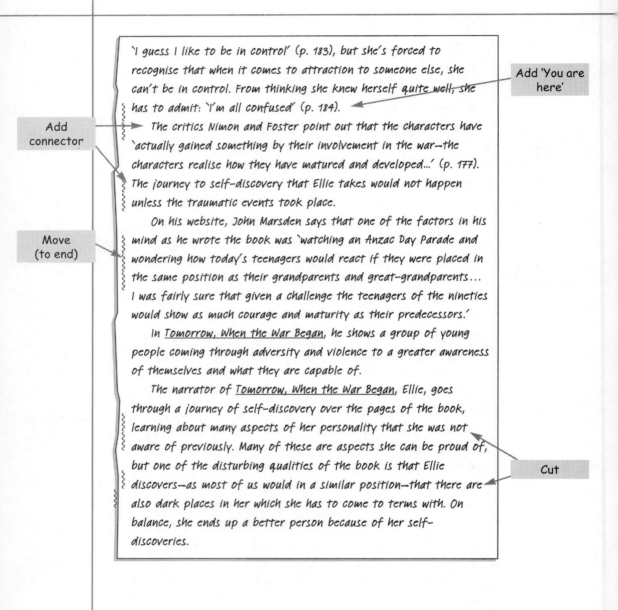

Add 'You are here'

'I guess I like to be in control' (p. 183), but she's forced to recognise that when it comes to attraction to someone else, she can't be in control. From thinking she knew herself quite well, she has to admit: 'I'm all confused' (p. 184).

Add connector

The critics Nimon and Foster point out that the characters have 'actually gained something by their involvement in the war—the characters realise how they have matured and developed...' (p. 177). The journey to self-discovery that Ellie takes would not happen unless the traumatic events took place.

Move (to end)

On his website, John Marsden says that one of the factors in his mind as he wrote the book was 'watching an Anzac Day Parade and wondering how today's teenagers would react if they were placed in the same position as their grandparents and great-grandparents... I was fairly sure that given a challenge the teenagers of the nineties would show as much courage and maturity as their predecessors.'

In Tomorrow, When the War Began, he shows a group of young people coming through adversity and violence to a greater awareness of themselves and what they are capable of.

The narrator of Tomorrow, When the War Began, Ellie, goes through a journey of self-discovery over the pages of the book, learning about many aspects of her personality that she was not aware of previously. Many of these are aspects she can be proud of, but one of the disturbing qualities of the book is that Ellie discovers—as most of us would in a similar position—that there are also dark places in her which she has to come to terms with. On balance, she ends up a better person because of her self-discoveries.

Cut

Second draft

Changes are shown in bold type.

'Self-discovery out of disaster'—this is the theme of <u>Tomorrow,</u> <u>When the War Began</u>, by John Marsden. The book is the story of a group of young people reacting to a major crisis—the invasion of Australia by an unnamed foreign power.

In the course of this book, the main character, Ellie, goes through several different kinds of self-discovery as she responds to the frightening and violent things that are happening around her.

'Self-discovery' is a concept with several meanings. The Macquarie Dictionary defines 'discovery' as 'To get knowledge of, learn of, or find out; gain sight or knowledge of something previously unseen or unknown.' Self-discovery, then, implies learning something previously unknown about yourself.

Self-discovery can mean learning good things about yourself, but it can also mean discovering things about yourself that are not so good.

One of Ellie's first moments of self-discovery is a positive one. It occurs soon after the teenagers come back from a camping trip and find their families have been locked up in the showground. They need to come out of the shadows to get close enough to see what's going on. Ellie is not sure she has the guts for this. She says: 'To come out of the darkness now would be to show courage of a type that I'd never had to show before. I had to search my own mind and body to find if there was a new part of me somewhere' (p. 81). Finally she brings herself to do so and says: 'I felt then, and still feel now, that I was transformed by those four steps...I started becoming someone else, a more complicated and capable person...' (p. 82).

Another positive self-discovery is her capacity for love. Over the course of the book, Ellie develops an interest in two of the boys in the group and is surprised by her feelings: 'It was all happening too unexpectedly...Lee was so intense he scared me, but at the same time I felt something strong when he was around—I just didn't know what it was' (p. 183).

Part of Ellie's maturation over the course of the book is her new awareness that the parent–child roles are reversed after the invasion. The book opens with all the young people trying to persuade their cautious parents to let them go on the camping trip. But as the reality of the invasion sinks in, Ellie wonders how her parents reacted when it happened. She says, 'I hoped they'd been sensible' (p. 78)—more often what a parent thinks about a child.

As well as these positive aspects of herself, Ellie also discovers a darker side. One of the first moments of violence in the book is when Ellie blows up three soldiers with a lawnmower. Telling the others about it, she says: 'I began to have trouble—It was hard for me to believe that I had probably just killed three people. It was too big a thing for me to get my mind around. I was so filled with horror. I felt guilty and ashamed about what had happened' (p. 95). In fact she thought she might have changed into 'a raging monster' (p. 161).

Another moment of self-discovery that Ellie finds disturbing is the fact that she thinks both Lee and Homer are attractive— 'I didn't have any plans to become the local slut...' (p. 161)—and tries to deny her feelings. She wants things to be simple and clearcut, and is disturbed by feeling attracted to both at once. From thinking she knew herself quite well, she has to admit: 'I'm all confused' (p. 184).

During the events of the book, Ellie is forced to get to know herself more deeply than ever before. The critics Nimon and Foster point out that the characters have 'actually gained something by their involvement in the war—the characters realise how they have matured and developed...' (p. 177). In this sense, although the events of the book are terrifying, the journey to self-discovery that Ellie takes might not happen unless the traumatic events took place.

Tomorrow, When the War Began is a good example of a book that provides a journey towards self-discovery for its main character. Ellie goes through a journey of self-discovery over the pages of the book, learning about many aspects of her personality that she can be proud of, but is also forced to recognise the dark places in herself.

On his website, John Marsden says that one of the factors in his mind as he wrote the book was 'watching an Anzac Day Parade and wondering how today's teenagers would react if they were placed in the same position as their grandparents and great-grandparents... I was fairly sure that given a challenge the teenagers of the nineties would show as much courage and maturity as their predecessors.'

In <u>Tomorrow, When the War Began</u>, he shows a group of young people coming through adversity and violence to a greater awareness of themselves and what they are capable of.

This is still only a 'draft'—I could revise it several more times and improve it quite a bit. However, even two drafts are better than one.

Revising an essay

1 Make a copy of the first draft

★ This is so you can scribble on this one to your heart's content.

★ Space it generously—then you can read it easily.

2 Read it through pretending that someone else wrote it

> Hint…read it in one go, as your readers will.

★ Don't stop and fix things.

★ If something sounds wrong, just mark it with a squiggle on this first reading.

★ Don't stop to work out *why* it sounds wrong.

3 Consider making cuts

Ask yourself:

★ Is this essay longer than required?

★ Have I padded it to make it up to length?

★ Have I waffled on pompously and got tangled up in long, complex sentences?

★ Have I repeated myself?

★ Have I included material that doesn't connect to the assignment?

If so, write CUT against each squiggle that flags repetition, long-windedness or irrelevance.

4 Consider adding something

Ask yourself:

★ Have I assumed that my readers know something I haven't actually said?

★ Have I left out a step in my argument?

★ Have I left out an important piece of information?

★ Have I failed to show *how* something is relevant to the topic?

★ Have I got ideas that seem disconnected, and need to be joined?

★ Have I failed to give supporting material for a point I've made?

★ Do I need to add a GOS or a GFS?

If so, write ADD.

> Hint...if you add too much, you can always take it out again later!

5 Consider moving parts around

Ask yourself:

★ Is this information relevant, but not in a logical sequence?

★ Is this idea relevant, but not a step in this particular argument?

★ Have I introduced information at the wrong time (too early, before its relevance can be shown: too late, after the reader needed it)?

★ For a two-pronged essay, have I chosen the best way of arranging the material (see page 89)?

Write MOVE against the parts that need it.

> Hint...
> sometimes a diagram helps.

6 What if you can see a problem but not how to fix it?

Ask yourself:

★ Is it that I can't bring myself to cut something out?
(Solution: tell yourself a little white lie: you'll find a place for it 'in a minute'.)

★ Is it that I can't think of anything to add?
(Solution: go back to the idea-starters in Step One, especially research. Also, go back to the assignment and read it again.)

Hint...this is why you made a copy before you started.

★ Am I afraid I'll get into a worse muddle when I move things around? (Solution: cut the essay up, physically, and spread the bits out on the table. Then sticky-tape the pieces together in the new order. Primitive, but it works!)

★ Are the ideas in the right order but still sound jerky? (Solution: use connecting phrases such as 'On the other hand...', 'In addition...'.)

★ Is it that I can't think of a GOS? (Solutions:

  – look for a brief, punchy quote to open with;

  – open with a question;

  – open with a dramatic contrast or contradiction.)

★ Is it that I can't think of a GFS? (Solutions:

  – If you haven't done so for a GOS, end with a strong quote;

  – refer back to the assignment—not by quoting the whole thing, but by using one or two words from it.)

Be prepared to have several attempts at a GOS and a GFS.

Recap

Your piece is in pretty good shape now. All it needs is a final polish—the last step!

STEP SIX

Editing

PERFECT PRESENTATION... it seems to MAKE EVERYthing taste Better!

What's in STEP SIX

About editing

If you were snatched away right now by aliens and never seen again, you'd still get a reasonable mark for your writing piece. It's got plenty of ideas, they're in the right order, and the whole thing flows without gaps or bulges.

However, in the event of an alien abduction it would be comforting to know that you'd left a really superior piece of writing behind. The way to achieve this is through the last step of the writing process: editing.

What is editing, exactly?

Basically 'editing' means making your piece as reader-friendly as possible by making the sentences flow in a clear, easy-to-read way. It also means bringing your piece of writing into line with accepted ways of using English: using the appropriate grammar for the purposes of the piece, appropriate punctuation and spelling, and appropriate paragraphing.

Why edit?

I've used the word 'appropriate' rather than 'correct' because language is a living, changing thing and the idea of it being 'right' or 'wrong' is less important than whether it suits its purpose… there's nothing wrong with those thongs, but maybe not for a job interview!

It's all about being practical. If you use spellings that aren't the usual ones, or grammar that isn't what we've come to accept as 'right', it will distract your readers. Instead of thinking 'what wonderful ideas this person has', they'll think 'this person can't spell'. It will break the trance of reading.

The final polish.

Re-invent spelling and grammar by all means…but not in an assignment!

Readers can be irritated and troubled by unconventional usage (I've had dozens of letters from readers about the fact that I don't use inverted commas around dialogue in some of my novels). It's your right to make up new ways to do things, but expect to pay a price for it. In the case of a school essay, this price might be a lower mark.

(Like everything else about the English language, there are exceptions to this. Imaginative writing often plays fast and loose with accepted ways of using English in order to achieve a particular effect.)

The read-through

As with revising, the first thing to do is to read the piece all the way through, looking for problems.

Make a note of where you think there are problems, but don't stop to fix them. Once you've *found* them all, you can go back and take your time *fixing* each one.

If there's even the slightest feeling in the back of your mind that something might not be quite right, don't try to talk yourself out of that feeling.

As writers, we all want our piece to be perfect, so we have a tendency to read it as if it is perfect, with a selective blindness for all its problems. For that reason, this is a good moment to ask someone else to look at it for you.

To make a piece as user-friendly as possible, you need to check the piece for **style**, **grammar** and **presentation**.

If you think something might be wrong...then it probably is.

Editing imaginative writing

Editing for style

As you wrote your imaginative writing piece, you may have found you were changing style or felt uncomfortable with the style you'd chosen. And there were probably times when you were not able to think of the perfect word or image.

This is normal and a sign that you had your priorities right: first get the basic shape of the piece right, then worry about getting every word perfect.

Now, however, is the moment to think of that 'exactly right' word, and to check that your style is appropriate for its purpose and has been applied consistently.

Questions to ask yourself about style

Is this the most effective style for this piece?

You might take into account the **content** of the piece (a funny, light-hearted piece will have a different style from a serious or emotionally intense piece). You might also think again about the likely **readers** of your piece, and which style will impress them most: you'd probably choose a different style for fellow students, a teacher you know well or an anonymous examiner who's never met you.

It's not too late to change style.

Have I stuck consistently to the style I chose?

Writing that slides around between formal and informal, slangy and pompous, can make the reader feel as if they're trying to listen to three different people all talking at once. Sometimes you can build up a sensitive or funny moment in a story and then, with a phrase in the wrong style, spoil the effect completely.

Does the writing give the reader a smooth ride or a bumpy one?

Sometimes the style of a particular sentence can be appropriate and consistent, but it can just sound awkward or be hard to follow. Sometimes individual sentences are okay, but the joins between them need smoothing out with connecting words or phrases.

Decisions about style for a piece of imaginative writing are never as clearcut as 'right' and 'wrong'. There's a subjective element here and that's why you might do several drafts—the best way to decide about style is to try a few. A choice of style might seem right in theory, but just sound wrong on the page.

To recap on what style means and how to choose the best one for your piece, go back to Step Four (page 103).

Editing for grammar

Grammar is a big subject, and for a proper understanding of it, I strongly suggest you get a specialised book about it. Read this brief summary below in conjunction with the 'User-friendly grammar' section at the end of this book.

Questions to ask about grammar

Is this really a complete sentence?

If not, it's a sentence fragment (see page 196).

Have I joined two complete sentences together with only a comma between them?

If you have, it's a run-on sentence (aka comma splice or fused sentence, see page 197).

Do my subjects agree with my verbs?

This is called subject–verb agreement (see page 198).

Try reading the piece aloud. If you stumble over something, change it.

A computer grammar check could be helpful.

Have I changed tense or person without meaning to?

This is where the writing starts in one tense but suddenly shifts into another tense ('I do this' to 'I did this', for example) or starts being about 'he' and slides into 'I' somewhere along the line (see page 199).

Is one bit of my sentence somehow attached to the wrong thing?

It could be a case of a dangling modifier—sounds weird, and it is (see page 200).

Have I put enough commas in? Or too many?

A comma's basic purpose in life is to indicate to the reader that there should be a slight pause in the sentence (see page 201).

Have I put apostrophes in the right places?

Apostrophes are those little misplaced raised commas that occur in the middle of some words such as 'they're' or 'it's' (see page 202).

If I've used colons and semicolons, have I used them properly?

A colon is ':' and a semicolon is ';' (see page 203).

If I've used inverted commas and brackets, have I used them properly?

You use inverted commas—'quote marks'—when you're quoting someone else's words exactly. This includes dialogue in imaginative writing and quotes in essays (see page 204).

Have I put paragraph breaks in the best places?

The basic rule for paragraphs is that every new idea should have a new paragraph. With imaginative writing this is often not clearcut—ideas tend to flow into each other. Follow the basic rule, and when you feel the ideas are taking a breath, or turning a corner, make a new paragraph.

In any case, don't let your paragraphs get too long. A new paragraph gives your reader a chance to catch up with you. As a very rough rule of thumb, if a paragraph is more than about eight lines long (typed), try to find a place to cut into it and make it into two separate paragraphs. It will 'lighten' the texture of your writing and make it easier on your readers.

Have I trusted the computer grammar checker too much?

Computer grammar checkers are useful, particularly to identify problems you mightn't have recognised. They're good at finding run-on sentences (they might call them 'comma splices') and sentence fragments.

However, you can't just apply their suggestions in every case. For a start, computer grammar checkers seem to hate the passive voice—but the passive voice is useful in essays and other forms of non-fiction writing. Also, the computer doesn't know what the purpose of your piece is, or who you're writing it for—so its suggestion may not be the best in your particular case. Use the grammar checker, but use your own judgement, too.

Computer grammar checks need to be taken with a pinch of salt.

Right NOW I'm bogged DOWN with EDITING, but I reckON I'LL HAVE finished iN time to go out TONight..

PreseNt TeNse—future perfect!

Editing for presentation

Presentation probably shouldn't matter, but let's face it, it does. Even if a story is inventive and imaginative and well written, if it's full of spelling mistakes and looks generally messy its reader will tend to be prejudiced against it.

Questions to ask about presentation

Is my spelling correct?

A spell checker on your computer will find most problems, but not all. In particular, it won't pick up spelling errors such as 'their' for 'there', since both of these are correct spellings—which one is right depends on the meaning of the whole sentence. It may also suggest US spellings, which aren't always the same as Australian ones, and it's not very good on proper names.

If you're not using a computer, go through your writing very carefully for spelling. If you have even the faintest shadow of doubt about the spelling of a word, look it up in a dictionary. There are certain words that all of us find hard—words like 'accommodation', 'necessary', 'disappoint'—so if you get to a word that you know is often a problem, double-check it even if you think it's right. Look also for consistency. Some words have two acceptable spellings—stick to the same spelling throughout your piece.

Another reader may pick up spelling errors and typos.

Have I got the best layout for my piece?

Layout means the way the text is arranged on the page. Layout makes a big psychological difference to your reader. A piece that's crammed tightly on the page with no space anywhere and few paragraphs breaks can look dense and uninviting. A piece that's irregular—with different spacing in different parts, different amounts of indentation, or different spacing between the lines—looks jerky and unsettling.

Teachers love writing comments and will be happier if you give them somewhere to do it.

Your layout should allow plenty of 'air' around the text—at least 1.5-centimetre margins all round, with more on the left-hand margin.

You should leave some space *between* the lines, too—not only for comments by the teacher, but also because your text is easier on the eye if there's good separation between the lines. Use a line-and-a-half space or double space on a computer.

Help your readers—double space your work!

It makes sense to have your piece as legible as possible. If you're handwriting your piece, take the time to form the letters clearly and make punctuation fully visible. Don't make your writing too small or too sloping. On a computer, use a clear, plain font (for example, New York or Times New Roman)—avoid fancy fonts. Use 10- or 12-point type size, no bigger or smaller.

Does this title help the reader?

The right title can be a big help to a piece of imaginative writing. Ideally, a title will be intriguing—teasing the reader to know what it's about. The ideal title should also carry within it the basic meaning of the whole piece. An overly obscure title can sound as if you're trying too hard. On the other hand you don't want to give away the whole story in the title.

The perfect title often comes when you've stopped trying to find it.

A time-honoured way to find a title is to go through the piece, looking for a significant word or phrase that will stand alone as a title. Another way, if you're as desperate as I often become trying to think of a good title, is to flip through books of poetry, or the lyrics of songs. They often have well-formed little phrases that resonate with meaning.

Editing imaginative writing

This is the first part of my imaginative writing piece with grammar and other mistakes added. (I did not include these mistakes in the earlier steps because they would have been distracting.)

Second draft

Run-on sentence	

It was getting so I was frightened of French classes. None of the other kids seemed to be having a problem, but I always felt stupid, we'd had three tests so far and I'd failed them all.

Punctuation

Run-on sentence	
Comma	

For a start, I just couldn't remember the words no matter how hard I tried. Plus, I hated having to pronounce the words in french, I knew they sounded clunky and awful.

Tense change

The French teacher let's call her Miss M is always very smartly dressed in little suites. Standing like a demonstration of `Good Posture`. Trying to look French her jacket was always just a bit too tight.

Spelling	
Sentence fragment	
Spelling	

We'd learned in Science about rats in cages where experimenters gave them electric shocks every time they turned on a light. After a while just the light was enough to make them squeel. Their were days when I felt like that—every Wenesday and Friday morning I woke up with a headache. The textbook didn't help. `All French nouns (persons or things) are considered either masculine or feminine, the noun markers "le" and "la" (often referred to as definite articles) indicating the category in a distinction usually known as gender.'

Dangling modifier

This is `le' and `la' business had me confused. I could eventually memorise the fact that maison meant house. A bit like mansion. But what about le and la? They both meant the, but le went with nouns that were called `masculine' and la went with words that were called `feminine'.

Punctuation

Punctuation	
Run-on sentence	

One day, I got up courage to ask Miss Marshall about it.

Miss Marshall, why is `leg' feminine and foot masculine? I asked.

I felt a little stirring in the class, everyone was thinking, Wow, what a dummie she is. Already I was sorry I'd asked. Miss Marshall smiled but it wasn't a friendly smile, or an understanding smile. To me it looked like a pitying smile.

Comma

`I'm afraid there just made that way `uise'.

Spelling

Editing imaginative writing

1 **Read the piece through**

★ Don't stop to fix mistakes, just mark them.

2 **Is the style okay?**

★ Have I chosen the **style** that's most entertaining for this piece?
(Think again about what style will most effectively engage the reader's feelings.)

★ Have I chosen **particular words** that jar with this style?
(Check for over-formal words in an otherwise casual style or the other way around.)

★ Have I chosen to construct **sentences** in a way that jars with the style?
(Be aware of complex 'literary' sentences in a conversational style.)

> Hint...if you're **aware** of the style, chances are it needs some work.

3 **Is the grammar okay?**

Ask yourself:

★ Have I written any **sentence fragments**?

★ Have I written any **run-on sentences**?

★ Do my **subjects agree** with my verbs?

★ Have I **changed tense** or person?

★ Have I **dangled** any **modifiers**?

★ Have I shown the pause I intended by using **commas**?

★ Have I used **apostrophes** in the right places?

★ Have I used **colons or semicolons** correctly?

★ Have I used **inverted commas or brackets** correctly?

★ Are there plenty of **paragraph breaks** and are they in the most natural places?

> More information on all these grammar points can be found on page 196.

Is the presentation okay?

Ask yourself:

★ Have I checked **spellings**?
(Be careful of sound-alikes such as their/there/they're.)

★ Is my **layout** orderly and well-spaced?

★ Have I found the best **title** for my piece?

Hint...this is a
good moment to
try it on a new
reader.

Stand back and shake yourself by the hand.
Your piece of writing is finished!

Editing an essay

Editing for style

You made a decision about style back at the start of Step Four, but in the heat of the moment as you wrote your draft, style might have slipped or changed. You might have forgotten a technical term, or been unable to think of the proper word for something, or you might have got your thoughts tangled up in long complicated sentences.

That's fine—that shows you had your priorities right: get the broad shape of the essay right first, not get bogged down in detail.

But now the moment has come to get to grips with all those details of style.

The main point about style in an essay is that it should always be the servant of meaning. In an essay, a style that draws attention to itself has failed. The aim of an essay is to get your ideas across strongly and clearly—the style is just the vehicle to convey the ideas.

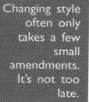

Changing style often only takes a few small amendments. It's not too late.

Questions to ask about style

Have I used the style most appropriate to an essay?

An essay should be written in a reasonably formal style. It should be in the third person or the passive voice. 'I' is generally not appropriate.

Have I chosen the most appropriate words for this style?

To achieve a formal style, individual words shouldn't be slangy or too casual. You'll be expected to use the proper technical terms where appropriate. On the other hand, your essay shouldn't be overloaded with pompous or obscure words. If a simple word does the job, use it.

Does the writing give the reader a smooth ride or a bumpy one?

In a first draft it's very easy to get yourself into long complicated sentences containing too many ideas. This is the time to simplify them. Even if a long complicated sentence is grammatically correct, it's generally awkward and hard to read. Try it out loud—if it's hard to get it right, or if it sounds clunky, rewrite it. It's much better to have two or three straightforward sentences than a big baggy monster.

On the other hand, the 'See Spot run' variety of sentence gets pretty mind-numbing after a while. If you have too many short, choppy sentences you may need to look at ways of connecting some of them, using words such as 'although', 'in addition', 'on the other hand'…

If all the sentences are constructed exactly the same way, you should look at ways of varying them.

Go back to Step Four to remind yourself about style.

Editing for grammar

Imaginative writing may have a little latitude with grammar, but an essay has none—the grammar just has to be right.

Grammar is a big subject, and for a proper understanding of it, I strongly suggest you get a specialised book on the subject. This is a quick checklist of some of the most common grammatical problems. You'll find a little more detail in the 'User-friendly grammar' section on page 196.

Read the essay aloud. If you stumble over something, change it!

Questions to ask about grammar

Is this really a complete sentence?

If not, it's a **sentence fragment** (see page 196).

Have I joined two complete sentences with only a comma between them?

If you have, it's a **run-on sentence** (aka **comma splice** or **fused sentence**) (see page 197).

Do my subjects agree with my verbs?

This is called **subject–verb agreement** (see page 198).

Have I changed tense or person without meaning to?

This is where the writing starts in one tense but suddenly shifts into another tense ('they do' to 'they did', for example) or starts being about 'he' and slides into 'I' somewhere along the line.

In an essay, you can decide whether to use the past tense or the present—whichever sounds most natural for your assignment. In the essay *Tomorrow, When the War Began*, I've used the present tense to describe the actions in the book. This is usual for an essay about literature—treating the story as if it's happening in the present. A history essay would normally be in the past tense (naturally enough).

Is one bit of my sentence somehow attached to the wrong thing?

This may be a case of **dangling modifier**—sounds weird, and it is (see page 200).

Have I put enough commas in? Or too many?

A comma's basic purpose in life is to indicate to the reader that there should be a slight pause in the sentence. This might be to separate the items in a list or to show which parts of a sentence belong together which as you can see if you took the commas out of this sentence might otherwise be a problem (see page 200).

Have I put apostrophes in the right places?

Apostrophes are those little misplaced raised commas that occur in the middle of some words such as 'they're' or 'it's' (see page 201).

If I've used colons and semicolons, have I used them properly?

A colon is ':' and a semicolon is ';' (see page 203).

If I've used inverted commas and brackets, have I used them properly?

You use inverted commas—'quote marks' when you're quoting someone else's words exactly. You also use them to talk about a word, not its meaning, as in *the word 'yellow' begins with 'y'*, or if you use a word in an unusual sense (see page 203).

Have I put paragraph breaks in the best places?

The basic rule for paragraphs is that every new idea should have a new paragraph.

If an idea is quite long, you might need to break it up into more than one paragraph. To do this, you'll need to find the 'sub-idea', or a sense of the idea changing direction—that will be the point at which to make a paragraph break. As a very rough rule-of-thumb, if a paragraph is more than about eight lines long (typed), make it into two separate paragraphs. It will 'lighten' the texture of your writing and make it easier on your readers.

Have I trusted the computer grammar checker too much?

Computer grammar checkers are useful, particularly to identify problems you mightn't have recognised. They're good at finding run-on sentences (they might call them 'comma splices') and sentence fragments.

However, you can't just apply their suggestions in every case. For a start, computer grammar checkers seem to hate the passive voice—but the passive voice is useful in essays and other forms of non-fiction writing. Also, the computer doesn't know what the purpose of your piece is, or who you're writing it for—so its suggestion may not be the best in your particular case. Use the grammar checker, but use your own judgement, too.

Computer grammar checks have to be taken with a pinch of salt.

Editing for presentation

Presentation probably shouldn't matter, but let's face it, it does. No matter how well-researched and clearly argued your essay is, it (and your mark) will be undermined by spelling mistakes, messy-looking layout or illegible handwriting.

Questions to ask about presentation

Is my spelling correct?

You'd think that using a computer spell checker would solve all spelling problems. However, if an incorrect spelling is in fact a legitimate word, the computer won't always pick it up as a mistake.

Use the computer spell check, but use your brain, too!

Be aware, also, that computer spell checkers may also suggest US spellings, which aren't always the same as Australian ones, and they are very bad at names of people and places.

If you're not using a computer, go through your writing very carefully for spelling. If you have even the faintest shadow of doubt about the spelling of a word, look it up in a dictionary. There are certain words that all of us find hard—words like 'accommodation', 'necessary', 'disappoint'—so if you get to a word that you know is often a problem, double-check it even if you think it's right. Another reader can also be a big help in picking up spelling errors. If there are two perfectly good spellings of a word, choose one and use it consistently.

Does my layout make my piece look good?

Layout means the way the text is arranged on the page. Layout makes a huge psychological difference to your reader. A piece that's crammed tightly on the page with no space anywhere and few paragraph breaks can look dense and uninviting. A piece that's irregular—different spacing on different parts, different amounts of indentation or different spacing between the lines—looks jerky and unsettling.

Your layout should allow plenty of 'air' around the text, with generous margins all round.

You should leave some space between the lines, too—not only for comments by the teacher, but also because your text is easier on the eye if there's good separation between the lines.

It's just human nature to prefer something pleasant to deal with and—contrary to some opinions—teachers are, in fact, human. So make sure your piece of writing is as legible as you can make it. If it's handwritten, write as clearly as you can and don't let the writing get too small or too sloping. On a computer, stick to one of the standard text fonts (New York or Times New Roman, for example). Don't use fancy fonts. Use 10- or 12-point type size. If your piece isn't long enough, the teacher won't be fooled by 16-point type. Human, yes. Entirely stupid—not usually.

Another reader might pick up spelling errors and typos.

Teachers love writing comments and will be happier if you give them somewhere to do it.

Help your readers— double space your work.

Does my title help the reader enter the essay?

Your essay may have a title: *The Water Cycle*. Or it may have a heading: *Term 2 assignment: 'What Were the Causes of World War I?'*. Whatever the title is, it should tell the reader exactly what the writing task is.

Have I acknowledged other people's contributions to my essay?

Most essay writers use other people's work to some extent. Sometimes they use it as background reading. Sometimes they specifically use information someone else has gathered or insights someone else has had. Sometimes they actually quote someone else's words.

It's very important to acknowledge this help, and say exactly where it comes from. This is partly simple gratitude, but it also means that other people can go and check your sources, to find out if, as you claim in your essay, Einstein really *did* say the earth was flat.

You should acknowledge other people's work in two ways: first, in a bibliography at the end of your essay. This is just a list of all the sources of information that you've used. List them alphabetically by author's surname, with information in this order: author, title, publisher and place and date of publication (or the address of the website).

As well as appearing in the bibliography, sources that you've used in a direct way should also be acknowledged in the essay itself—for example, 'As Bloggs points out, Einstein was not always right.'

The titles of any books that you refer to should be in *italics* (if you're using a computer) or <u>underlined</u> (if you're writing by hand).

Using other people's work without crediting them is plagiarism— you'll be heavily penalised.

Editing an essay

This is the first part of my essay with some grammar and spelling problems added. I did not include them in earlier steps because they would have been distracting.

Second draft

| | | Punctuation |

'Self-discovery out of disaster'—this is the theme of Tomorrow, When the War Began, by John Marsden. Reacting to a major crisis, the invasion of Australia by an unnamed foreign power, the book is the story of a group of young people.

Dangling modifier

Run-on sentence

It may not be true that all stories show a journey to self-discovery, In the course of this book the main character Ellie goes through several different kinds of self-discovery. Responding to the frightening and violent things that are happening around her.

Sentence fragment

'Self-discovery' is a concept with several meanings, the Macquarie dictionary defines 'discovery' as 'To get knowledge of, learn of, or find out; gain sight or knowledge of something previously unseen or unknown.' Self-discovery then implies learning something previously unknown about yourself.

Comma

Run-on sentence

Self-discovery can mean learning good things about yourself, it can also mean discovering things about yourself that are not so good.

Run-on sentence

Comma Use

One of Ellie's first moments of self-discovery is a positive one. It occurs soon after the teenagers come back from a camping trip and find their families have been locked up in the showground, they need to come out of the shadows to get close enough to see what's going on. Ellie is not sure she has the guts for this. She says: 'To come out of the darkness now would be to show courage of a type that I'd never had to show before. I had to search my own mind and body to find if there was a new part of me somewhere' (p. 81). Finally she brings herself to do so and says, 'I felt then, and still feel now, that I was transformed by those four steps...I started becoming someone else, a more complicated and capable person...' (p. 82).

Inappropriate word choice

Another positive self-discovery is her capacity for love. Developing an interest in two of the boys in the group the book shows Ellie being surprised by her feelings: 'It was all happening so unexpectedly...Lee was so intense he scared me, but at the same time I felt something strong when he was around—I first didn't know what it was' (p. 183).

Dangling modifier

Editing an essay

1 Read the piece through

★ Don't stop to fix mistakes, just mark them.

2 Is the style okay?

Ask yourself:

★ Have I chosen the style that's most appropriate for an essay?
(Remember, an essay is aiming to persuade or inform.)

★ Have I chosen **particular words** that jar with this style?
(Check for over-casual, conversational words or 'ordinary' words where a technical one would be more appropriate.)

★ Have I chosen to construct **sentences** in a way that jars with the style?
(Look for short, simplistic sentences, also for needlessly pretentious ones.)

> Hint...if you're **aware** of the style, chances are it needs some work.

3 Is the grammar okay?

Ask yourself:

★ Have I written any **sentence fragments**?

★ Have I written any **run-on sentences**?

★ Do my **subjects agree** with my verbs?

★ Have I **changed tense** or person?

★ Have I dangled any **modifiers**?

★ Have I shown the pause I intended by using **commas**?

★ Have I used **apostrophes** in the right places?

★ Have I used **colons or semicolons** correctly?

★ Have I used **inverted commas or brackets** correctly?

★ Are there plenty of **paragraph breaks**, and are they in the most natural places?

> More information on all these grammar points is found on page 196.

4 **Is the presentation okay?**

Ask yourself:

★ Have I checked spellings? (Be careful of sound-alikes such as their/there/they're.)

★ Is my layout orderly and well spaced?

★ Have I found the best title for my piece, which prepares the reader for the essay?

★ Have I acknowledged sources of ideas and information in a bibliography?

> Hint...this is a good moment to try it on a new reader.

Stand back and shake yourself by the hand.
Your piece of writing is finished!

Other useful stuff

At the beginning of this book I made the ambitious claim that the 'Six Steps' method can be applied to any kind of writing you might be asked to do. In this section, I'll support that claim.

Many kinds of writing...

So far, we've looked in detail at imaginative writing pieces and essays. But there's no end to the kinds of writing you'll be expected to know about or produce for school, university, work, interests or pleasure. Here are some of the most common:

- ★ procedures;
- ★ reports;
- ★ recounts;

- ★ personal responses;
- ★ biographies;
- ★ autobiographies.

Then there are:

- ★ letters;
- ★ speeches;
- ★ newsletters;
- ★ job applications;
- ★ references;

- ★ sales reports;
- ★ overhead or datashow presentations;
- ★ websites;
- ★ submissions.

Not to mention: the back of the soup tin and the box the toothpaste came in...

One way to do it

It would be impossible to memorise the formula for every kind of writing in the world. But if you memorise the Six Steps, you can adapt them to even the most out-of-the-ordinary writing job you might have to do.

Step One: Getting ideas

No matter what kind of writing you have to do, you should start by gathering together all the things you can think of about the subject. The simplest way to do this is just to list them straight down the page, in whatever order they come to you.

If you think you can do this in your head, that's fine. But that means your brain has to remember what you've already thought of, at the same time as thinking up new ideas. Personally, my brain works better when it only has to do one thing at a time.

Step Two: Choosing

When you look back over it, this list will probably contain a few things that you won't use after all. Perhaps they're not relevant, perhaps they're not polite, perhaps they're confidential. Whatever the reason, you can cross them off your list.

Step Three: Outlining

Every piece of writing is like a journey. It starts at the **Beginning**, travels along through the **Middle**, and **End**s up at its destination. It doesn't just hop around randomly—it's a sequence, from A through B to C.

Step Three is where you put your ideas into a sequence. The sequence is more or less the same for all kinds of writing.

Beginning

Every piece of writing has some type of an introduction: 'Reader, I'd like you to meet my piece of writing.' The Beginning might be:

> Congratulations on purchasing the Whizz-bang Toaster. Please take a moment to review its features.

Or:

> Dear Auntie May,
>
> I'm sorry it's been so long since I wrote to you, but I want to thank you for sending me a birthday present.

Or:

> Ladies and Gentlemen, Welcome to the Fourth Annual General meeting of the WoopWoop Pigeon-Fanciers Society. Tonight I'd like to talk to you about the pigeon as a foodstuff.

Or:

> Dear Sir / Madam,
>
> I would like to apply for the position of Chief Bottle-Washer with your firm. I feel I am ideally suited to this position because of my good track record in washing bottles over the last few years.

You get the idea. Whatever form the Beginning takes, it sets you up to get on with the Middle.

Middle

The Middle is the whole reason the piece of writing exists. It's where you tell the reader whatever it is you want them to hear. The Middle usually contains a number of different ideas—so you have to work out some kind of easy-to-follow sequence for these.

The Middle might be the instructions for the Whizz-bang Toaster, from steps one to ten.

It might be telling Auntie May how much you like her present, how you've always wanted one just like it, and what you plan to do with it in the holidays.

It might be telling your audience how to make Pigeon Pie, Pigeonburger or Pigeon Pavlova.

It might be the details of all the bottle-washing you've ever done, plus your experience in washing pots, pans, knives and forks.

When you've said everything you want to say, the end of your journey is in sight.

End

At the end of a journey you slow down, look around you, work out where you are. It's the same with writing. In one way or another, you wind down, and leave your reader gently rather than abruptly. An End might be:

> If you experience problems with your Whizz-bang Toaster, call us toll-free on 1800 000 000.

Or:

> Well, that's it for now. Thanks again for the great present and take care. Best wishes, Sylvester.

Or:

> If you'd like to buy my book, *A Thousand Ways to Cook a Pigeon*, I'll be selling copies at the table over there in a few minutes. Thank you for your attention, ladies and gentlemen, and good pigeon-fancying.

Or:

> As you'll see from the above, my qualifications for the job of Chief Bottle-Washer are excellent. I feel sure I have a great deal to offer your firm. Please let me know if I can give you any further information.
>
> Yours faithfully,
> Sylvester Smith.

Some kinds of writing don't have much of an End (newspaper reports, for example). However, in that case, the Middle is arranged in such a way as to give a tapering-away feeling to the end (usually, by arranging the information in the piece from the most important or dramatic to the least important). Just about every kind of writing needs something to indicate to the reader that the piece has actually come to an end, not just that a page is missing.

Step Four: Writing

This is where you follow your Beginning, Middle, End outline of ideas and flesh them out to give yourself a first draft.

Step Five: Revising

You go through your first draft looking for big structural problems—places where you've left something out, places where you've put too much in, or places where things are in the wrong order.

Step Six: Editing

You go through the piece again, looking for all those little niggly things that give a piece of writing a bad name—grammar and spelling mistakes, messy layout and presentation that makes the piece hard to read.

Types of texts at a glance

Text type	Purpose	Structure
Narrative	To tell a story	Orientation (who, where, when) Complication (need for action) Evaluation (response by characters) Resolution
Recount	To tell about a series of events happening one after the other	Orientation (who, where, when) Record of events Reorientation (reason for recount)
Report	To give information	General statement Descriptions (of different aspects of the topic)
Review	To assess the value of an art work	Context (background to art work plus a synopsis) Description (of characters, key events, style) Judgement (balance of strengths and weaknesses)
Historical recount/ account	To write about events of the past	Background (general information about the period) Record of events (in sequence) Evaluation (of the significance of the period)
Procedural recount	To record a procedure	Aim (scientific purpose) Record of events (what was done) Results (what happened) Conclusion (what was found, even if nothing)
Exposition	To argue for a point of view	Thesis Arguments supporting thesis Restatement of thesis
Discussion	To discuss both sides of an argument	Introduction of issue (both sides) Arguments for one side Arguments for other side Judgement

Tense	Voice	Style
Past or present	First or third person	Formal or casual
Past	First or third person	Formal or casual
Past or present	Third person	Formal
Present	First or third person	Formal or casual
Past	Third person	Formal
Past	First person or passive voice	Formal
Present	Third person	Formal
Present	Third person	Formal

User-friendly grammar

Here are some common grammar problems mentioned in Step Six and some advice on how to fix them.

Sentence fragments

A sentence fragment is a sentence that's not really complete. When we talk, we often use sentence fragments because we can usually work out what's meant if a bit is left off. But in written English— particularly essay writing—they're not usually appropriate.

A complete sentence must have a **subject** (someone or something doing something in the sentence), and a **full verb** (showing an action or a state of being). Most sentences also have an object: something that the verb is being 'done to'. For example:

I (subject) **love** (verb) pancakes (object).

Sometimes a sentence can *seem* to have a subject and verb but not really have one. For example:

Running for the bus.

This sentence might look as though 'the bus' is the subject of the sentence, and 'running' is the verb. The problem is that 'running' isn't a complete verb—it needs another bit of verb to make it complete—'am running' or 'was running'. Also, it's not the bus that's running. In fact, the person doing the running isn't in the sentence at all. That means that this fragment doesn't have a **subject**.

Getting a grip on exactly why all this is so takes a fairly thorough understanding of grammar. I recommend you gain this, but in the meantime there are a few practical strategies you can apply to a piece of writing.

Beware of sentences that start with an 'ing' word. Check that they are not sentence fragments. If they are, there are two ways to fix them:

1. Get a subject into the sentence and complete the verb:

    He was running for the bus.

2. Join this sentence fragment onto another complete sentence that gives it a subject and contains a full verb.

    Running for the bus, he tripped over.

Run-on sentences

You might meet these under the name of **comma splices** or **fused sentences**. What these names mean is that several complete sentences have been stuck together without any properly certified joining devices. Imaginative writing might be able to get away with run-on sentences, especially in dialogue. On the whole, though, you'd be safer to avoid them.

Here's an example:

I love writing essays, it makes me feel good.

There are two complete sentences here, each with a subject and a whole verb. Sentence number 1 is : 'I (**subject**) love (**verb**) writing essays.' Sentence number 2 is: 'It (**subject**) makes (**verb**) me feel good.'

In English you're not supposed to just stick two sentences together without the proper glue between them. Why not? Well, let's just say that's the way it is, like genders in French.

When you're editing your writing, be on the lookout for long sentences with several parts. If each individual part could stand on its own, and you've just stuck them together with a comma, you've got to do something. There are two main ways of fixing run-on sentences:

1. Make two separate sentences by putting a full stop where you had a comma.

   I love writing essays. It makes me feel good.

2. Join the complete sentences with a licensed 'joining word' (or conjunction). These are words such as 'and', 'but', 'because', 'however' and so on.

   I love writing essays and it makes me feel good.

   Or:

   I love writing essays because it makes me feel good.

Subject–verb agreement

If you remember our discussion of complete sentences, you might have noticed that the subject and the verb **agreed**. In fact, one of the markers of a subject is that it controls the verb—or rather, the form that the verb will take.

I (subject) **love** (verb)

you **love**

he **loves**

she **loves**

we **love**

they **love**

You can see that some of these have an 's' on the end and some don't. Whether you add one or not depends on which subject you're using.

Some verbs are even trickier, using a completely different word with different subjects:

I **am**

you **are**

he **is**

she **is**

we **are**

you **are**

they **are**

And some are very simple. Most past-tense verbs don't change at all:

I **lived**

you **lived**

he **lived**

she **lived**

we **lived**

you **lived**

they **lived**

For those whose first language is English, subject–verb agreement is usually instinctive—it just 'sounds right' (although even native speakers can get it wrong, too). If English isn't your first language, it's something that has to be checked carefully.

You might, possibly, use deliberate non-agreement of subject and verb in imaginative writing—in dialogue, for example. However, as with all these grammatical errors, it's probably safest to avoid them for school and university writing jobs. If you *do* use them, you need to be able to justify them in terms of the overall meaning of the piece.

Changes of tense or person

It's easy to start a piece of writing in the past tense but find somewhere along the line that you've slid into the present tense—or the other way round. It's also easy to start using 'he' but somewhere along the line start talking about 'I' instead.

This is disorienting for a reader.

There are times with imaginative writing where you might deliberately change tense. (For example, switching to the present tense can make an incident more dramatic.) The important thing is to do it on purpose, for a reason that you can justify.

Dangling modifiers

Sound weird, and dangling modifiers sound weird in writing, too.

This is when you've got a sentence with several parts to it, and one of the parts 'modifies' another part but it's in the wrong place. The modifying bit 'dangles' in space, attaching itself, in desperation, to anything nearby. For example:

Enjoying a meal of worms, Sylvester watched the birds.

'Enjoying a meal of worms' belongs with 'the birds'—it tells you about them, or modifies them. However, because of the order of the sentence, the modifier has come unstuck from 'the birds', and seems to be attached to poor old 'Sylvester'.

Dangling modifiers usually sound ridiculous. The reader may laugh—but at the *writer*, not the *story*.

Dangling modifiers can usually be fixed by rearranging the sentence so that the modifier is right next to the thing it's modifying:

Sylvester watched the birds enjoying a meal of worms.

However, if you have a very snarled-up sentence, full of dangling bits everywhere, it's usually easier to take it apart and make it into two separate sentences.

Commas

A comma's basic purpose in life is to indicate to the reader that there should be a slight pause in the sentence.

Sometimes commas separate items in a list. The last two items of a list should already be separated by the word 'and', so you don't need a comma there.

I took bread, milk, eggs and cheese.

Commas are handy to set off a little side-thought in a sentence—
the same way a pair of brackets (parentheses) would. (If you want
to get technical, these are called 'parenthetical commas'.) In this
case you need to use a pair of them, on either side of the
thought—just as you'd use a pair of brackets:

> My friend Sandy, who was a high-jump champion, never
> forgot my birthday.

Or:

> My friend Chris, however, never remembered anything.

The danger zone with commas is when you've got two complete
sentences (see run-on sentences above), and you join them together
with nothing more substantial than a comma. It's like using
sticky-tape to mend the fence. Something more substantial is a
semicolon (;). This is discussed more below.

Apostrophes

These are those little misplaced commas that occur in the middle of
some words, such 'they're' or 'it's'.

There's a lot of confusion about apostrophes. They've got two
main uses:

* ★ They're used to indicate that something has been taken out
  of a word—for example, the apostrophe in 'they're' indicates
  that this is a shortening (or contraction) of 'they are'. The
  apostrophe tells the reader that the letter 'a' has been
  dropped. If it wasn't there, the word would look like some
  weird Olde Englishe word: 'theyre'.

* ★ They're also used to show ownership—for example, 'the
  girl's hat'. In this case, the job that the apostrophe does is to
  tell the reader that the hat is owned by someone—that is,
  the girl.

In this second case, the apostrophe signals a difference between 'girl's' (indicating that the girl owns something) and 'girls' (indicating more than one girl). Often, we don't really need this signal—it's usually pretty clear from the context which one is meant, and in spoken English there *is* no difference.

However, the apostrophe becomes useful when there is more than one owner. When there is more than one owner, we put the apostrophe after the 's'.

The girls' dog bit me.

This is telling us that more than one girl owns the dog (probably sisters, down the street, in the yellow house, with that rooster that crows first thing in the morning…).

So, the general rule about apostrophes is this: if it shows that a letter has been taken out or if it shows ownership, use an apostrophe. If it doesn't show one of these things, don't use it.

So far so good. But the problem is the exception to this rule: the word 'its'. In the case of 'its' the rules overlap. As a shortened form of 'it is', it ought to have an apostrophe to show that a letter has been removed. That would make it 'it's'.

But if 'it' owns something, it should also have an apostrophe. That would make it 'it's' in that case, too.

This overlap of meanings has been solved by everyone agreeing on this solution: when the apostrophe is used, it means 'it is'. When the apostrophe is not used, it means 'ownership'.

For example:

It's a fine day today. (short for 'it is')

The dog bit its tail. (showing ownership)

In practical terms: resist the temptation to insert an apostrophe in any old word ending in 's'. If the 's' is there just to make the word plural, it doesn't need an apostrophe. If it's there to indicate ownership go right ahead (but check that there's not more than one owner; then the apostrophe goes after the 's').

Look carefully at every use of 'it's' or 'its'. If it's short for 'it is', use the apostrophe. Otherwise, don't.

Colons and semicolons

A colon is ':' and a semicolon is ';'.

A semicolon is a legitimate joining device for two complete sentences, and therefore a 'cure' for a run-on sentence.

The colon has several common uses. It can be used to introduce a list:

> As she ran out of the house she grabbed all her things: her hat, her bag, her glasses and her keys.

Or it can be used to introduce an important or dramatic word:

> All my attention was focused on one object: the door.

A colon is usually the right way to introduce a quotation:

> Buddha said: 'This too shall pass.'

Punctuation with inverted commas and parentheses

You use inverted commas—'quote marks' with dialogue. Parentheses (commonly called 'brackets') are often handy, too, when you want to add a little bit extra to the main point and tack it onto the sentence. The question is, where does the punctuation go—inside the inverted commas or parentheses, or outside them?

Generally, the rule is that the punctuation goes inside the inverted commas or the parentheses, if there's a complete thought inside them.

For example:

> 'Hey Bill!' he shouted.
>
> He sat down (on a chair with no seat!) and fell straight on the floor.

However, if the thought is completed *outside* the inverted commas or brackets, then the punctuation should be outside them, too. For example:

> I bought some bread (the grainy kind), some olives and some cheese.

Paragraphs

The basic rule for paragraphs is that every new idea or subject should have a new paragraph. This is not always as simple as it sounds because ideas tend to flow into each other. Follow the basic rule and when you feel your writing is taking a breath, or the idea is turning a corner, give it a new paragraph.

In any case, don't let your paragraphs get too long. A new paragraph gives your reader a chance to take a breath. As a very rough rule of thumb, if a paragraph is more than about eight or ten lines long (typed), try to find a place to cut into it and make it into two paragraphs. It will 'lighten' the look of your writing and make it easier on your readers.

Pronoun reference and agreement

A pronoun is a word that stands in the place of a noun. Without pronouns, writing would get very repetitive (for example, you would have to use a character's name every time you mentioned them, instead of the 'he' or 'she').

What can happen with pronouns when you're writing, though, is that the link between the noun and the pronoun can get broken, and then the reader isn't clear what the pronoun is referring to. For example, the sentence might use a pronoun that doesn't match the original noun:

When **a dog** sees food, **they** are pleased.

The noun is singular (only one dog) but the pronoun is plural ('they').

This problem often arises in English because of the need to avoid gender-specific language—English doesn't have a singular pronoun that includes both males and females—we only have 'he' or 'she', so people now sometimes use 'they'.

When a student gets a good mark, they are pleased.

This is becoming accepted, but if you feel uncomfortable about it there are two solutions:

1. You can keep the singular noun and use both singular pronouns:

   When **a student** gets a good mark, **he or she** is pleased.

2. Or, less cumbersomely, you can make the noun a plural so that you can keep the plural pronoun:

   When **students** get good marks, **they** are pleased.

Ten-minute exam kit

Under stress—in an exam or with a deadline looming—it's easy to panic about writing and forget the many details in a 'how-to-write' book. So here is a no-frills summary of each step. When the pressure is on, you can remind yourself quickly what to do.

Step One: Getting ideas

1. Underline

★ the **task** word (or phrase) in your writing assignment (the one telling you what kind of piece to write);

★ the **limiting** word (or phrase) in your writing assignment (the one telling you what kind of focus is required).

2. List

★ Write down anything you can think of about the subject of the assignment.

★ This should include any thoughts about the subject that pop into your head, plus any dates and names you've crammed.

★ Just a word or two will be enough for each thought—use a new line for each.

★ Aim for a minimum of ten items on your list before you stop and read them over.

Step Two: Choosing

Look at your list from Step One. Think about the **purpose** of your piece and **test** your ideas against it.

1. What's the purpose of this piece of writing?

Is it:

★ to entertain?

★ to persuade?

★ to inform?

2. Test each idea from Step One

If your purpose is to entertain, ask:

★ Can I use this to make the reader feel something (the **feeling** test)?

★ Can I use this as part of an ongoing storyline (the **story** test)?

★ Can I use this to let the reader *see* what's happening (the **description** test)?

If your purpose is to persuade or inform, ask:

★ Can I use this to convey information to the reader (the **information** test)?

★ Can I use this as an idea or theory about the topic (the **concept** test)?

★ Can I use this as an example, or to support a point of view (the **evidence** test)?

3. If an idea doesn't pass the tests for your purpose, cross it off the list

Step Three: Outlining

You've got a list of useful ideas from Step Two. Here's what to do next:

1. Sort your ideas into Beginning, Middle or End

Ask yourself:

★ Can I use this in the Beginning, as introductory scene-setting?
(If you can, write 'B' beside it.)

★ Can I use this in the Middle, as development and filling-out of the idea?
(If you can, write 'M' beside it.)

★ Can I use this in the End, as a winding up?
(If you can, write 'E' beside it.)

2. Number the ideas in each of these categories

Ask yourself:

★ What is the most logical (or most interesting) order for all the Bs? For all the Ms? For all the Es? Give them numbers: B1, B2, etc.

3. Add to your outline if there are gaps in it

Ask yourself:

★ Is there a gap in the logical sequence of information or ideas?

★ Is there a gap in the balance of the piece? (Should I have arguments *for* as well as *against*, or is there too much *setting* and not enough *incident*?)

★ Is there a gap at the Beginning or the End? (Write a one-sentence 'summary'.)

Give the new ideas a tag (for example, B1a, B1b) to show where they should be inserted into the outline.

Step Four: Drafting

You've got a list of all the ideas you're going to use, with tags to tell you what order they should go in. Now, decide on a **style** and **write** each idea out.

1. **Style depends on what your piece is aiming to do and who it's being written for**

   Ask yourself:

   ★ Would a formal style suit my purpose and audience best?

   ★ Would a casual style suit my purpose and audience best?

2. **Write out each numbered item from Step Three in sentences**

   Some will only need one sentence, while others will expand into several.

   Your 'summary' card will be the basis for your thesis sentence. As a rule of thumb, each item in the Middle will be a new paragraph.

   Don't get bogged down making one bit perfect—it's better to sketch in all your ideas, no matter how badly, than to have just one or two beautiful paragraphs and then nothing else.

   You now have a first draft. If you've left yourself a few minutes to spare, you can fix up some of the rough parts of this draft.

Step Five: Revising

You've got a first draft and a few minutes to fix the worst of its faults. Here's what you do now: Cut, Add and Move (CAM).

1. Should I cut anything?

★ Is this bit relevant to the assignment?

★ Have I said the same thing twice?

★ (For imaginative writing) is this bit preventing the story being interesting?

2. Should I add anything?

★ Have I *shown* why each idea is relevant to the assignment?

★ Have I assumed my reader knows something I haven't told them?

★ Have I left out something that would help the piece achieve its purpose (evidence, vivid details...)?

★ Could I smooth the joins between the ideas by adding connecting phrases?

3. Should I move anything?

★ Is there a feeling of jumping backwards and forwards?

★ Is this a good idea in itself, but doesn't seem to relate to the ideas around it?

Now your piece should flow smoothly, with no gaps, bulges or tangles. If you've got time for Step Six, you can work on the grammar, spelling and presentation.

Step Six: Editing

You've got a piece with everything in it, and it's all in the right order. If you've got a few minutes left, here's how to make it look its best:

Check the style, the grammar and spelling.

I. Is the style okay?

★ Are the word choices and sentence structures appropriate for the purpose of the piece?

★ Are they appropriate for the intended reader?

★ Can I smooth the joins between sentences with connecting words or phrases?

★ Are some sentences clumsy or over-complicated?

2. Is the grammar okay?

★ Is this a complete sentence? (Does it have a subject and a full verb?)

★ Is this really two sentences stuck together with only a comma?

★ Have I changed tense without meaning to?

3. Is the presentation okay?

★ Have I spelled the name of this real person or country or chemical correctly?

★ Have I spelled the characters' or author's names correctly?

★ Have I spelled technical or special words correctly?

Congratulations. You can be confident that you've shown what you know about the subject, and that you've presented it in the best way.

Bibliography

Crew, Gary and Libby Hathorn, *Dear Venny, Dear Saffron*, Lothian Fiction, Melbourne, 1999

Frost, Robert, 'Mending Wall' in *The Norton Anthology of Poetry*, edited by M. Ferguson, M.J. Salter and J. Stallworthy, 4th edition, W.B. Norton & Company, 1996

Macquarie Dictionary, 1st edition, The Macquarie Library, Macquarie University, 1981

Marchetta, Melina, *Looking for Alibrandi*, Puffin Books, Ringwood, Victoria, 1992

Marsden, John, *Tomorrow, When the War Began*, Pan Australia, Sydney, 1995

Nimon, Maureen and John Foster, *The Adolescent Novel: Australian Perspectives*, Centre for Information Studies, Wagga Wagga, NSW, 1997

Townsend, Sue, *The Secret Diary of Adrian Mole, Aged 13¾*, Methuen, London, 1980

Twain, Mark, *Huckleberry Finn*, Collins, London, 1953

Wyndham, John, *The Day of the Triffids*, Penguin, London, 1961

Acknowledgements

A big thank you, first of all, to all the teachers of writing I was lucky enough to encounter early on. Mrs Linney at North Sydney Demonstration School and Mary Armstrong at Cremorne Girls' High School were the first in a long line of imaginative teachers of writing. They taught me that writing isn't magic: up to a point, it's something you can learn how to do, and the learning can be fun.

Apart from my teachers, my students have taught me most about writing. Thank you, all those I've had the pleasure and privilege of working with over the last fifteen years of writing classes.

A number of high school teachers were kind enough to read this book at draft stage and make invaluable comments and suggestions, especially Debra Kelliher, who gave generously of her time, and whose astute, insightful comments saved me from many follies and gave me new ideas. Many thanks also to Lyn Power, Marcia Shepherd, Su Lengker and Marie Cullen, who read the book in draft form, and to Kerry Edmeades, Mal Garrett, Garry Collins, Cathy Sly, Beverly Hayes and Eva Gold, who responded constructively to the original idea. Thank you also to those involved in English teachers' conferences in several states, who participated so generously during the workshops at which I gave the Six Step process its trial run.

Great thanks go to John Marsden for his kindness in letting me use his book *Tomorrow, When the War Began* as the subject for my essay writing examples.

I tried out this book on two young writers who were in a position to be quite frank with me: a special thank you, Tom and Alice Petty, for being the guinea pigs.

Index